Keep on Rollin'

The Complete Guide

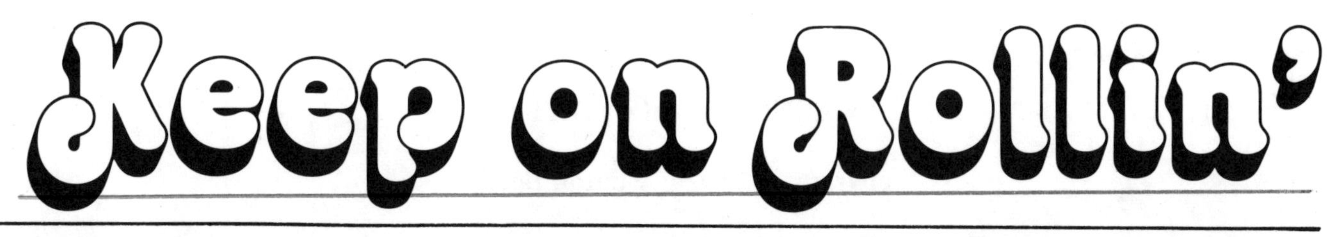

To Roller-Skating in America

By Sharon Boorstin

A Warner Communications Company

WARNER BOOKS EDITION

Book design by Marsha Eva Gold.

Design assistants: Michael Feiner and Anita Arliss

ISBN 0-446-87811-1

Rollerskates on front cover appear courtesy of

Cheapskates-Sure-Grip Skate Company.

Warner Books, Inc., 75 Rockefeller Plaza, New York, N.Y. 10019

A Warner Communications Company

Printed in the United States of America

Not associated with Warner Press, Inc., of Anderson, Indiana

First Printing: September, 1978

10 9 8 7 6 5 4 3 2 1

Bruce Hazelton

Table of Contents:

Introduction

It all began back in the 18th century, when a clever sports enthusiast in Holland invented a warm-weather substitute for ice-skating. The first roller rink in the United States opened over a hundred years ago, and by the 1920s, the same kids who cheered Babe Ruth were strapping metal wheels to their Buster Browns, to take off down the block with an ear-splitting roar.

Today, a new roller revolution is rumbling across America: skate manufacturers have sold more pairs in the last five years than they did in the twenty before, and conservative estimates indicate that an impressive 4000 roller rinks span the country. From boardwalks along the Pacific, through climate-controlled skate centers in Midwestern towns, to throbbing, big-city roller discos, and on suburban sidewalks everywhere, children, teenagers, and adults—over thirty million strong—are gliding along on person-powered wheels.

Why this renewed fascination for roller-skating—a fad that has swelled into a full-scale boom? Technological breakthroughs provide one clue: in the late '60s, polyurethane wheels (responsible for the current skateboard craze), created a roller skate that for the first time provided a whisper-quiet, smooth-as-velvet ride; and by 1970, drafty old barn-like roller rinks, once echoing with an out-of-tune organ, started to give way to plush arenas where skaters could sail over satiny epoxy-covered floors, moving to the stereo beat of top forty hits. In addition, adults began to discover the healthful benefits of this sport/recreation; without having to battle the elements, or suffer the knee-jolting pain of jogging, skaters can burn up to 360 calories an hour.

Many find roller-skating more than a fun way to fight their flab or rock out on Saturday night. Competitive skating is serious business: modern precision skates enable experts to spin faster and jump higher than ice skaters, and fans can look forward to marveling at wheeling feats for the first time in the 1984 summer Olympics.

Keep on Rollin' invites readers to make the most of the skate fever sweeping the country: besides a detailed description of the latest in skating equipment, it explains why and how roller-skating is good for your health and includes a chapter on "Exerskating"—exercises you can do on skates that will work wonders for your figure. It takes a lively look at skaters pursuing their passion—on the Venice, California, boardwalk; in a roller rink; a skateboard park; under the strobe lights of a roller disco; and before the judges at a tense competitive meet. In addition, *Keep On Rollin'* is a how-to book, featuring diagrams, illustrations, and photographs explaining how to execute roller-skating techniques, from a beginner's first glide to the aspiring pro's fancy jump turn.

In short, *Keep On Rollin'* shows how to get the most out of roller-skating—as sport, as exercise, and as fun. From the teenagers who head for the rink every day after school to the adults about to lace up their first pair of skates in thirty years, *Keep On Rollin'* is everyone's *Complete Guide to Roller-Skating In America.*

Chapter I

Re-Inventing the

Rolling Through History

Wheel

Library of Congress

We've come a long way since steel disks grated on sidewalks . . .

The hollow rumble of Kryptonic wheels in Central Park. Roller "hot-doggers" backwards-skating on a glistening rink in Omaha, or slaloming along a Pacific Ocean boardwalk. We've come a long way since steel disks grated on sidewalks—even longer since a legendary 18th-century Dutchman nailed large spools to wooden strips and fastened them to his feet, inventing a summer substitute for ice-skating. Today, with over 4,000 rinks—and an outdoor skating renaissance—roller-skating has swelled into a full-scale American craze.

RE-INVENTING THE WHEEL

But the development of skating was not always so smooth. Few people realize what a long and bumpy road roller-skating has taken since that clever Hollander felt the first thrill of man-powered wheels. How many adventurers back then indulged in the sport we don't know, but the chroniclers of roller history blame Joseph Merlin, a Belgian inventor who dazzled Londoners with his creations in 1760, for putting the fledgling entertainment on the oddball list. Perhaps Mr. Merlin was a better musician than skater, but when he showed up at a masquerade gala on homemade metal skates, playing his hand-crafted violin, he couldn't control his aim, let alone stop, once he got rolling. He crashed full-speed-ahead into a wall, smashing a $1300 mirror to smithereens, totaling his violin, and nearly killing himself.

Chicago Skate Company

Library of Congress

Library of Congress

Sioux City Public Museum

Library of Congress

Skating in roller palaces was popular before the turn of the century. Once streets became paved, skaters took to the open road.

(far left) In 1865, William Fuller skated before curious crowds around the world.

Library of Congress

Chicago Skate Company

No one showed much enthusiasm for roller-skating after Mr. Merlin's downfall until a Frenchman, in 1819, patented his own roller invention. Monsieur Pettibled's devices imitated ice skates down to having rollers of wood, metal, or "deluxe" ivory, arranged in a straight line. He claimed one could match an ice skater's maneuverability with his roller skates, but in truth, rounding a corner, not to mention cutting a figure eight, was impossible. Robert John Tyers, an English inventor around the same period, tried solving the problem by making the center wheel in the line larger than the others. But when the skater shifted his weight forward or back to turn, he was left with only *two* wheels' support—a tricky feat of balance, even for those light on their feet. The steadier, but no less awkward, Austrian tricycle skate, was a flop as well.

Finally, in the 1840s, a Berlin tavern gave roller-skating a much-needed shot in the arm, advertising "pretty waitresses on roller skates." The *London Illustrated News* reported that the girls dazzled customers not only with their looks, but also with their ability to

Sioux City Public Museum

Roller palaces became popular meeting places in the 1880s.

skate to the tables "with any number of pint pots of beer in both hands, without disturbing a single flake of froth." From there, roller-skating soared all the way into culture: Meyerbeer's opera, *Le Prophète*, opened at the Paris Opera House in 1849, the entire cast performing a simulated winter ice-skating sequence on wheels. When the company toured Europe, their roller-skating made bigger headlines than their singing—perhaps because more often than not, a member of the cast would roll off the edge of the stage into the orchestra pit (in London, one cast member had to be rescued from the middle of a bass drum.)

YANKEES PUT ROLLER-SKATING OVER THE TOP

In 1865, one American single-handedly carried the art of roller-skaing to the far corners of the globe: William Fuller performed a comic act on roller skates before maharajahs in India, Egyptians in Suez, and Russians in Odessa and Moscow. His show in St. Petersburg sometimes attracted as many as five hundred enthusiasts, who, after the performance, skated along with him in the public gardens.

Around the time Fuller introduced roller-skating to foreign lands, another enterprising

Library of Congress

Library of Congress

Skates quickly advanced from the Plympton "rocking skate" to high fashion boots for ladies.

Yankee was responsible for bringing the sport to the American public—and making it stick. In 1863, James Leonard Plimpton patented his "rocking skate" (as it was nicknamed by Charles Dickens, describing it in a London paper), and its basic design is still applied to the roller skates of today. With four boxwood wheels—aligned two in front and two in back—and rubber cushions between the plate and the wheels, skaters could maneuver curves by simply leaning to one side or the other.

As innovative as Plimpton's skate was, the smashing success of roller-skating was more the result of Plimpton's flair for publicity than of the invention itself. For Plimpton wanted the whole world to share in his new creation. He built a lavish $100,000 rink in the heart of Manhattan, creating a popular social gathering place. And soon thereafter, he made all the papers by inviting the "right people" to the gala premier of his fashionable roller palace in Newport, Rhode Island. Then he set out to conquer the world—touring the nation to open luxurious rinks with polished wooden floors, and teaching new and intriguing skating techniques. Cards and letters poured in praising his inventiveness. L. P. Yandell, a Louisville clergyman and physician, touted roller-skating as the greatest social innovation of the age, writing to Plimpton:

Chicago Skate Company

"No conception has ever entered the human mind, in this century, so important to the health of young people in our cities as this skating within doors. Nothing could exceed it in grace. Nightly, tastefully dressed young men and girls, sail, swim, and float through the mazes of the march, as if impelled by magic power. The old people assemble to witness the sight, apparently as much delighted as their children. All honor, I say, to the originator of Roller Skating. Long may he live. The children will rise up and bless his name."

SKATING TAKES OFF

In the 1880s, the industrial revolution boosted roller-skating into the national consciousness, making the sport as accessible and popular as bicycling. Before then, skaters had to build their own, or buy a hand-fashioned wood or metal pair. Now, assembly lines turned out thousands of pairs of inexpensive, long-wearing skates. Fragile boxwood wheels gave way to sturdy steel rollers, and soon, ball-bearings made them even more maneuverable.

Big-city roller palaces in America and England drew hundreds of skaters daily, where adults paid a quarter, kids under twelve only a dime, to skate to the oom-pah-pahs of lively 30-piece bands. The roller rink became a recreational center for people of all ages and all social classes. The Casino Rink in Chicago attracted 5000 skaters to its 1884 grand opening, and English aristocrats flocked to an *all-marble* rink in London. In the prim Victorian age, there could be no more perfect spot for a gentleman to escort a lady to than a roller parlor. As a New York newspaper reported when the Olympian Roller Skating Rink opened on Broadway: "The youth of today, instead of spending his evenings in playing pool or drinking, can now be seen wheeling around the skating floor with some lady companion, and instead of coming from

Chicago Skate Company

In 1929, roller-racing made it to Madison Square Garden.

his sport with callow and whitened complexion; he emerges from this exhilarating exercise with the glow of health in every feature." Skating became a spectator sport as well: roller polo was so popular, urban leagues vied throughout the East, and roller speed tourneys drew fans eager to bet on a winner.

THE ROLLING TWENTIES

Facing new competition, the cavernous roller rinks had their ups and downs after the turn of the century. With the development of daring new entertainments—movies, the Charleston, and the automobile—by the Roaring Twenties, the drafty palaces were nearly empty. Then, ironically, skating got a second lease on life: as city streets were paved, *outdoor* skating flourished on the wide-open concrete spaces. New York City sponsored roller-skating speed tournaments, with events ranging from the 100-yard dash to the 880, and roller hockey teams competed on playgrounds for a shot at the annual city championships in Central Park. Some skaters took to the open road: Arthur Allegretti rolled from Buffalo to New York City in 1927, covering the 500 miles in 58 hours straight, with only an occasional stop at roadside stands to fill up on hot dogs and grape soda. In 1929, roller-skating finally made it to Madison Square Garden, with 16 three-man teams skating a non-stop marathon: one man per squad raced while his partners rested in bunks set beside the track. By the fourth day, only half the teams were left in the race, and spectators crowded in to cheer on the five bone-weary crews that made it across the finish line. The winners logged 1246 miles and eight laps—in six days!

Fancy trick skating of the 1920s found its place in vaudeville, with acts like the Crystal

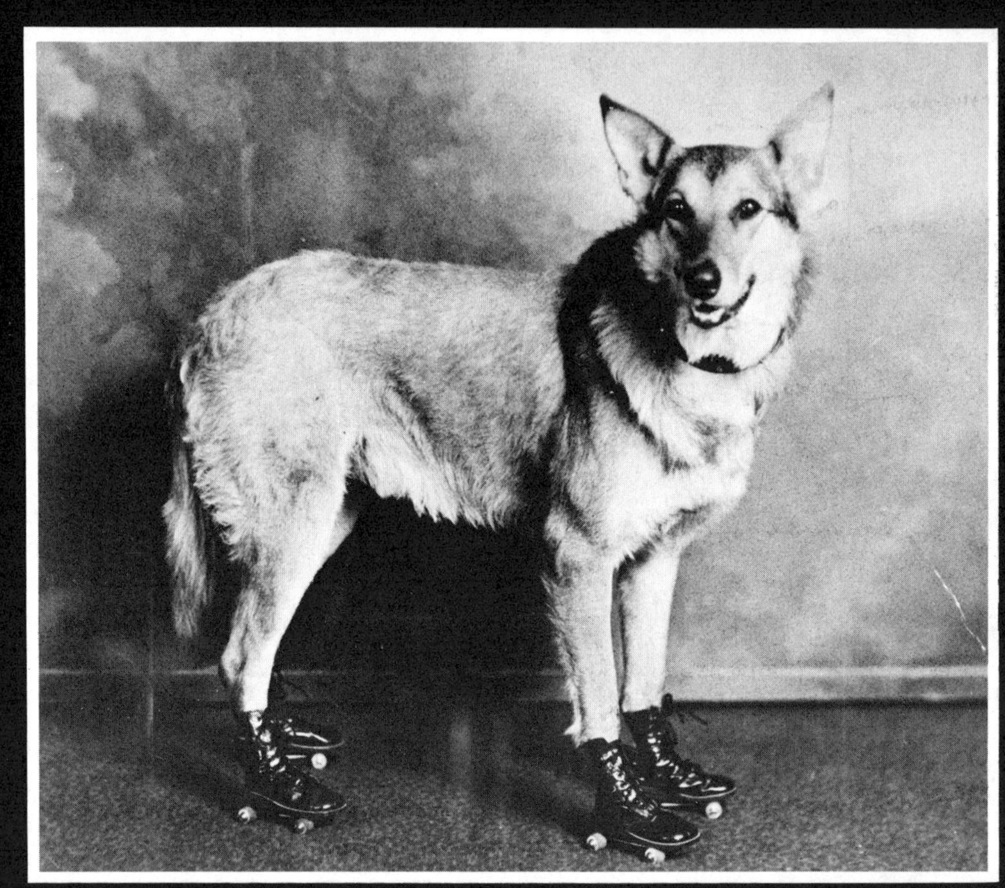

Chicago Skate Co.

Roller-skating found its way into vaudeville.

Chicago Skate Co.

Trio—"Defying the laws of gravitation, they'll thrill you with their fast skating and daring spins!" As advertised, Babe, Barney, and Joe pulled off airplane spins, around-the-neck spins, and flip-over spins, on the 15-foot portable wood floor they lugged around the country with them. They toured from the Big Apple, through small Midwestern towns, all the way to Hollywood, where they attained a measure of stardom doing their act in a Warner Brothers silent hit: *Domestic Troubles*.

NEW UPS AND DOWNS

With the Depression, down-and-out Americans returned to roller rinks in droves for an economical entertainment that let them skate away their woes without spending money they didn't have. Fred Astaire and Ginger Rogers added a note of glamour to the sport, stunning moviegoers with a gliding-and-tapping dance number on skates to Gershwin's "Let's Call the Whole Thing Off" in the 1937 film *Shall We Dance?* In 1938, the English dance and figure-skating team of Jimmy and Joan Listone introduced competitive dance-skating to this country, dazzling with graceful precision routines to organ waltzes, marches, and tangos. Soon thereafter, serious roller-skating enthusiasts organized the first U.S. National Dance and Figure Roller Skating Championships.

The Forties brought an era of big bands, the swing, and extravagant roller-skating shows with all the glitter and pizzazz of a Busby Berkeley musical. The "Roller Skating Vanities" entertained audiences from Madison Square Garden to opera houses and high school auditoriums all over the country. And with World War II, the Government joined the roller-skating bandwagon, as the head of Physical Fitness for Civil Defense touted its healthful benefits: "Those who are engaged in roller-skating are better fitted to prosecute the war." Even Eleanor Roosevelt is reported to have tried it.

But the '50s and '60s found skating

Ninety-nines Inc.

Amelia Earhart was one of the many who roller-skated during the Thirties.

back in a slump. The roller-skating carhop was a minor innovation that came and went with the drive-in restaurant. And basically, roller rinks, once glamorous social centers, were deteriorating into run-down hangouts where tough guys went to pick up the wrong kind of girl on a Saturday night. Competitive skating continued to attract serious freestylers and racers—in fact, it grew, slowly and steadily. But all that most Americans knew of skating was the rough-and-tumble Roller Derby that bombarded them nightly with bone-crushing televised skating histrionics.

TODAY—GANGBUSTERS

So how did we get from Roller Derby to Roller Disco, from prim skating parlors to plush skating pleasuredomes? Why the burgeoning enthusiasm for skating that has taken the country by storm since the early 1970s? For starters, in the late '60s, new urethane wheels (responsible for the current skateboard craze) created a roller skate that for the first time provided a whisper-quiet, smooth-as-velvet ride, enabling skaters to maneuver with greater ease and precision than ever before. Since the 1970s, when Americans began showing a heightened concern with staying fit, skating has become an "in" form of exercise. And today, keeping up with the times, drafty old barn-like rinks that once echoed with an out-of-tune organ have given way to space-age fantasylands where skaters sail over satiny, epoxy-covered floors to the throbbing stereo rhythm of the latest hits.

Now, roller-skating has even gone far beyond the friendly neighborhood roller rink. In the 1979 Pan American Games, it will take its rightful place among other international spectator sports, and not long thereafter, skilled roller skaters for the first time will be vying for Olympic gold medals.

Call it a fad, the latest in popular recreation, or a full-fledged cultural craze, but today, roller-skating—for young and for old—is definitely *what's happening.*

Jerry Nista

The Forties was an era of roller-skating extravaganzas.

Author of *Keep On Rollin'* and her dog, Darwin, invent a new way to enjoy roller-skating.

Paul Boorstin

Chapter 2

From Cheap Skates To Holy

Equipping the Complete Skater

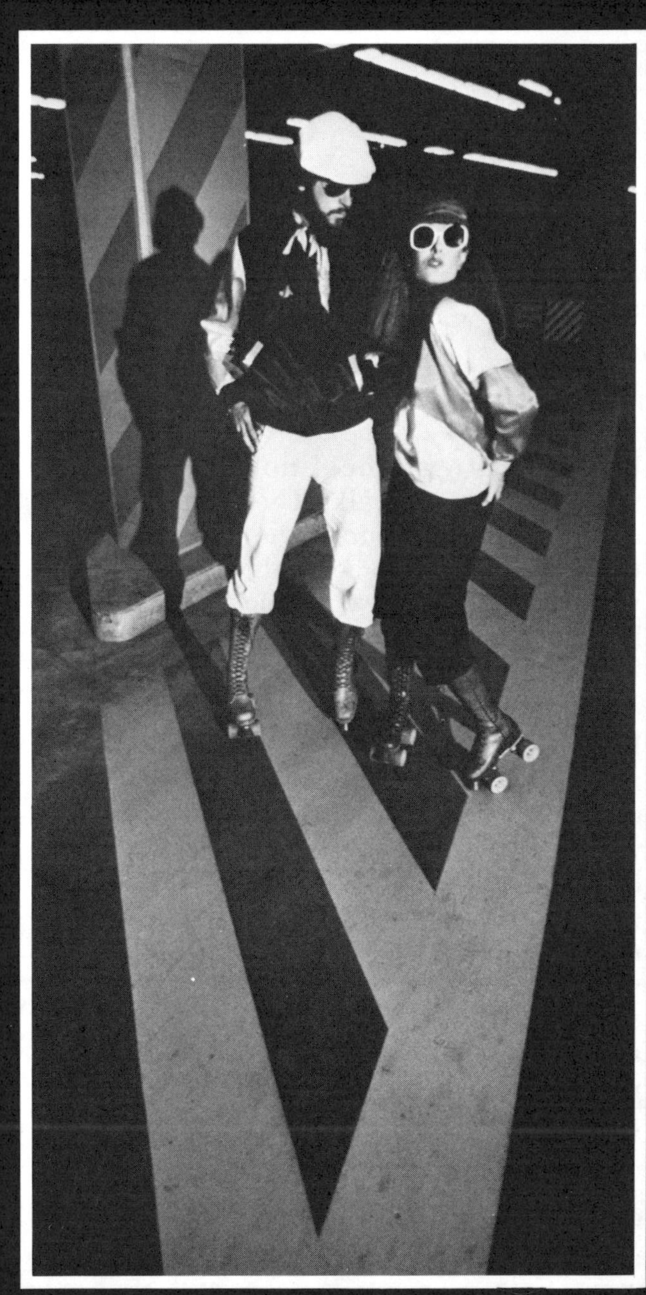

Cheapskates

Rollers

Roller skaters wheel noiselessly along the Venice boardwalk. Their rented skates glide on hard polyurethane wheels, for the rental shops here stock outdoor skates with wheels that will give a smooth ride on the bumpy asphalt and will *last*—withstanding users' spills in the sand, mud puddle splashes, and believe it or not, dashes through the surf (much to the shops' dismay!).

But some veteran roller renters would gladly pay extra for skates with bigger, *softer* wheels—if there are any pairs left. The shops have to charge more for these deluxe soft wheels: not only do they cost *five times* as much as the harder wheels, they last only *half* as long. Still... *the softer the wheels, the softer the ride.* But only on concrete or asphalt! If you skated with these same soft wheels in a roller rink, you could end up slipping and breaking your neck!

Confusing? Fortunately, unlike most sports (including skateboarding), where you have to buy your own equipment, skating can be enjoyed without ever having to know the difference between the dozens of kinds of gear on sale today. It's possible to rent a perfectly adequate pair at the boardwalk or rink for less than it costs in gasoline to drive there in the first place. In fact, one of the great attractions of roller-skating is that it can be very economical.

But once you're hooked on skating, you may want to *buy* your very own pair of skates. Then the confusion begins. At Sears, you can get sidewalk skates for as little as $12.95, rink skates for $22. Or you can combine the best in leather boots with an expensive plate and super-deluxe wheels costing over $10 apiece (that's $80 just for the wheels), and end up shelling out over $200!

The possibilities—the combinations of skate features—can boggle the mind and slenderize the pocketbook. The best way to choose the perfect skate for you is to decide:

1. *Where* you plan to skate (outdoors, or at a rink).
2. *How* you plan to use them (recreation or competition).
3. *What* you are willing to spend.

IT BEGINS WITH THE WHEEL

The story of today's roller-skate wheels is inextricably wound up with skateboarding. In fact, skateboarding was born back in the Fifties when someone thought of putting *roller-skate wheels* on a surfboard! Young would-be surfers rode the concrete waves in their neighborhoods, but the spills were more frequent than the thrills, and the craze died out—just as outdoor roller-skating reached a standstill around the same time. Why? The old-style hard composition wheels were just *too hard* for either sport: the ride they offered was too bumpy and dangerous on city sidewalks.

Then, during the late '60s, polyurethane, a durable plastic, was molded into roller-skate wheels which were softer and

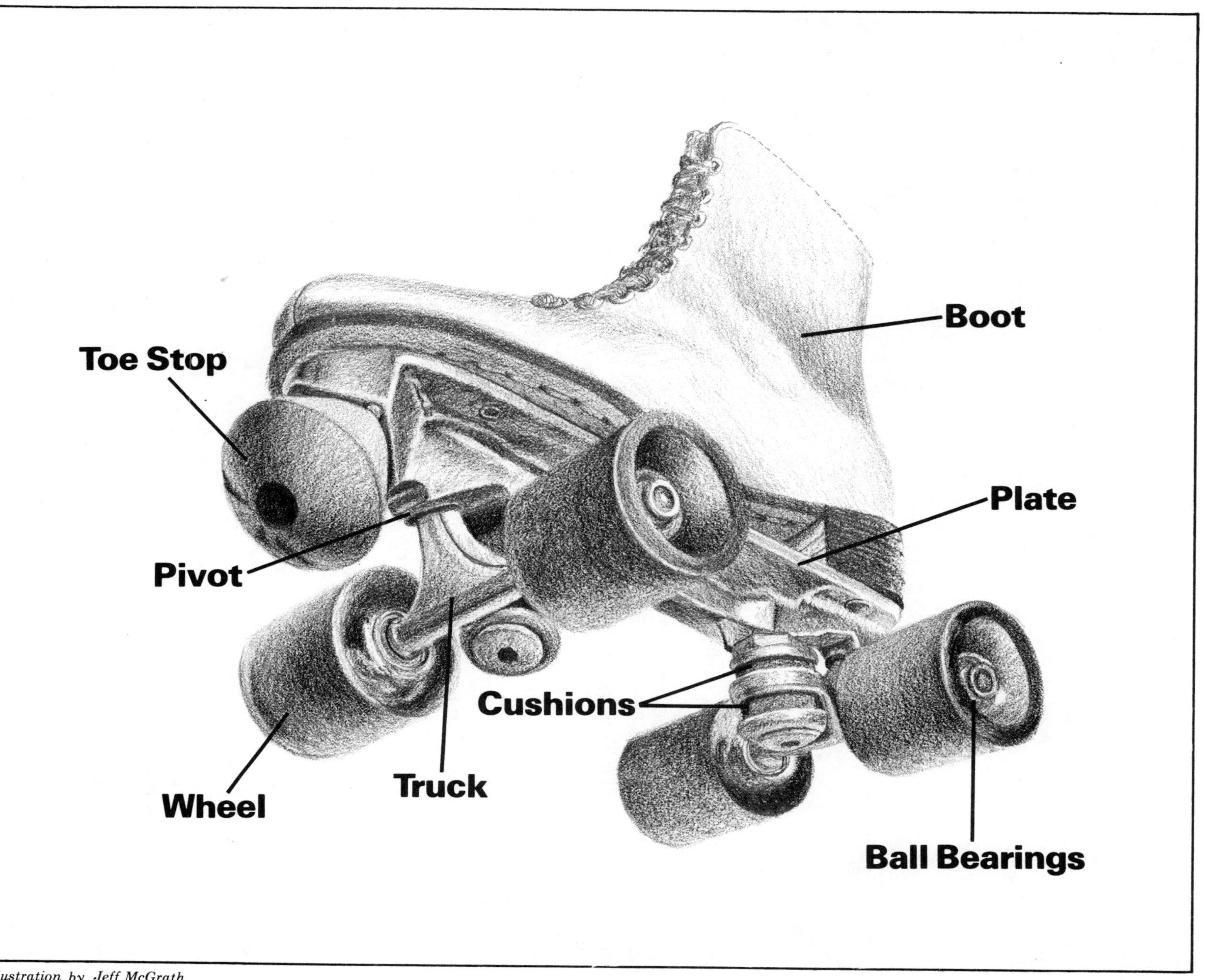

Illustration by Jeff McGrath

Cheapskates

The modern roller skate is a far cry from the wooden-wheeled skates of the 1880s.

gripped better on uneven surfaces. Though they were too slippery on smooth roller rink surfaces, they were perfect for bumpy outdoor surfaces and gave new life to skateboarding—and outdoor roller-skating—this time for good!

Today, polyurethane wheels have been developed to suit every purpose, place, and pocketbook. In addition to *soft* polyurethane wheels, an even more recent innovation, *hard* polyurethane and combination polyurethane-plastic composition wheels allow for surer grip and greater maneuverability on *rinks* than the old indoor wheels.

Now you can choose from a cornucopia of roller-skate wheels: some grip better than others; some roll faster and slide easier. Others wear longer, while others provide a soft, smooth ride.

CHOOSING AN OUTDOOR ROLLER-SKATE WHEEL

Skating over concrete on soft polyurethane wheels as opposed to hard composition wheels can be like riding in a Ferrari equipped with wide oval ties, instead of bouncing along in a Model T.

CLIMAX PARK ROLLER SKATES.

The Roller Skates represented by this cut are manufactured of the best material, and nicely finished in ebonized wood, strapped complete with patent buckles, nickel plated heel band, steel axles and malleable iron castings, having bearings one inch in length, which effectually prevents the wearing out by constant friction as is the case with other low priced roller skates. The axles revolve in the hanger bearings, and the wheels revolve on the axles, thus doing away with the friction that is common with other roller skates. A patent for these axles and bearings on roller skates was granted April 26, 1881.

Sizes of Skates, 7, 7 1-2, 8, 8 1-2, 9, 9 1-2, 10, 10 1-2, 11, 11 1-2 inches.
Price, per pair, with Ebonized Woods, Boxwood Rolls, $1.75.

THE NEW YORK ROLLER SKATES.

These roller skates are manufactured of the best materials, and nicely finished with French polished beech wood tops, strapped complete, with patent buckles, maple wheels and nickel plated heel bands. The wheels are hung to the tops in a simple and effectual way. The hangers have a middle support, which adds much to the strength and but little to the weight. This keeps the wheels apart, and makes a separate axle for each wheel. They are "light weight," perfectly strong and thoroughly reliable.

7 to 11 1-2 inches. **Price, per pair, $1.00.**

A. G. SPALDING & BROS., 108 MADISON STREET, CHICAGO.

Library of Congress

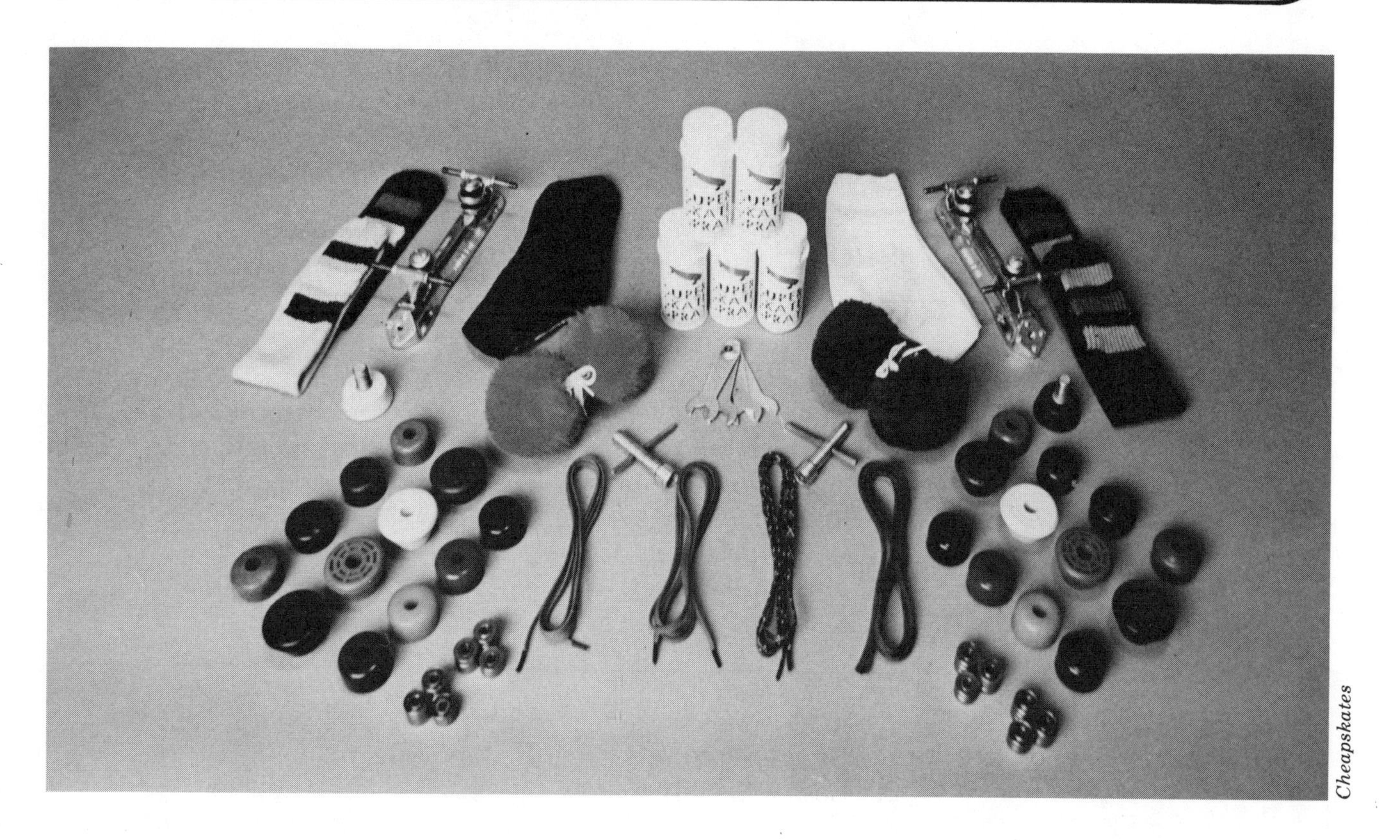

Cheapskates

The combination of possible skate features boggles the mind.

Polyurethane outdoor roller-skate wheels are often interchangeable with skateboard wheels, and they vary widely in *softness* (test a wheel's flexibility by squeezing it in your hand), *width* (from 60 mm to 70 mm), and *price*. A super-wide, super-soft wheel may cost three times as much as a harder, smaller wheel, and it may wear out twice as fast.

To pick and choose an outdoor roller-skate wheel wisely, consider the pros and cons on page 32.

OUTDOOR WHEELS DON'T MAKE IT INDOORS

Don't tote your 70 mm butter-soft polyurethane wheels into the rink on Saturday night and expect the manager to greet you with open arms. All the grit and grime embedded in the wheels would chew up his floor. He might be willing to let you skate if he has honed and buffed them down first, but that would wear down your wheels even more quickly than under normal outdoor skating conditions.

For wheels adaptable to both the sidewalk and the rink, stick to *hard polyurethane.* They'll resist street grime and be safer and more maneuverable than soft wheels on smooth indoor skating surfaces.

STRICTLY INDOOR SKATES

At roller rinks across the country, skates come free with the price of admission. And they're all alike—usually leather boot skates with wheels of hard polyurethane, or hard plastic composition, or a combination of both substances.

Hard wheels are slippery on rough outdoor skating surfaces because they can't touch the ground at all points. But indoors, particu-

	PROS	CONS
Softer wheel	1. Smoother, quieter ride. 2. Absorbs shock of pebbles and cracks in road. 3. Better gripping on uneven surfaces.	1. Costs more. 2. Wears out more quickly. 3. *Too* soft means a slower ride.
Harder wheel	1. Longer-lasting. 2. Less expensive. 3. Faster. 4. More versatile: can be used indoors or out. 5. Better for artistic skating.	1. Noisier. 2. May be slippery on uneven surfaces. 3. Gives a hard ride on uneven surfaces.
Wide wheel	1. Rolls faster with less skater effort over long distances. 2. If wide *and* soft, most comfortable ride on bumpy surfaces.	1. Clumsy for spins and artistic skating. 2. More expensive.
Narrow wheel	1. Better for spins and artistic skating. 2. Less expensive.	1. Slower and requires more skater effort in long runs.

Cheapskates

The soft polyurethane wheel revolutionized outdoor skating.

larly on the new, epoxy-slicked rink floors, they grip the smooth surface and provide good control.

For the recreational rink skater, whose repertoire of skating tricks may never go beyond skating backwards, rental skates are fine. But if you plan to learn artistic skating, buying roller skates to suit your particular needs becomes essential. Today, a competitive skater going to a meet may take as many as ten sets of wheels in varying sizes and flexibilities for the different events he is entering. He may take an array of trucks and boots also.

Freestyle and dance skates are likely to have heavier trucks—with an extra bar for added support—to withstand the stress of spins and jumps. The rubber cushions in the trucks may also be larger than those on regular skates.

Racing skates have support bars drilled with holes to minimize weight and allow for greater speed. Wheels are harder and lighter—often of wood, for less friction and more speed on smooth surfaces. Racing skates usually come with harder axles and racing cones.

BALL BEARINGS KEEP THE WHEELS ROLLING

Each skate wheel turns on two sets of ball bearings—usually eight each: steel balls 3/16″ in diameter. *Loose ball bearings* are the most inexpensive variety in general use today. They will give a smooth, adequate ride, except perhaps at high speeds. Their disadvantages: they collect grime, require frequent cleaning, and wear out sooner than *precision* bearings.

Closed, precision ball bearings, often packed in grease and connected with metal or nylon thread, are sealed with metal shields on

"Roller Chic": from hand-painted skate boot covers to silver lamé.

one or both sides. Precision bearings last longer than loose bearings, and may never need cleaning. However, they're double the price.

THE TRUCK: WHERE THE "ACTION" IS

The *truck* is the triangular piece of metal housing the axle that attaches your wheels to the skate boot plate. With its rubber cushions and pivot arms front and back, the truck performs three vital functions: in addition to linking the wheels to the boot, it absorbs shock, and most important, allows the skater to turn by applying pressure to his skate edges.

At one time, skates had all-metal trucks, without rubber pads to cushion the ride and provide good maneuverability. Now, you can buy skates with one cushion ("single action") or two cushions ("double action"), or in addition to the cushions, with rubber pads at the pivot points, providing "triple action" maneuverability. The degree of flexibility the truck can provide increases with the number of rubber cushions—and so does the price.

Adjusting your trucks

The *looser* the truck, the more the skate will respond to *body lean*. The *tighter* the truck, the greater the skate's stability. A beginning skater is advised to start with his trucks *tight*, until his ankles and calves are strong enough to maneuver easily and support his body without buckling. As the skater improves and his legs strengthen, the trucks can be loosened.

To tighten or loosen the rubber cushions in the truck, use an axle wrench to adjust the *action bolt* that holds them in place.

Here is how to judge whether your trucks should be loose or tight:

Tighter trucks:
1. For beginning skaters.
2. For heavy skaters whose weight alone would exert enough pressure on the edges for turning.
3. For good stability in jumps.

Looser trucks:
1. For expert skaters.
2. For lighter skaters who need to apply more body lean in turning.
3. For performing spins and complicated sequences in competitive skating.

PICKING YOUR SKATE BOOT IS EASY

Skate boots range from unlined vinyl, cheapest of all, to sturdy, all-leather boots. Some of the latest skate boots are made of nylon and vinyl, like those used in ice hockey, designed for greater lightness and speed.

If you want to be "different," Cheapskates in Venice, California, will mount

Cheapskates

Cheapskates

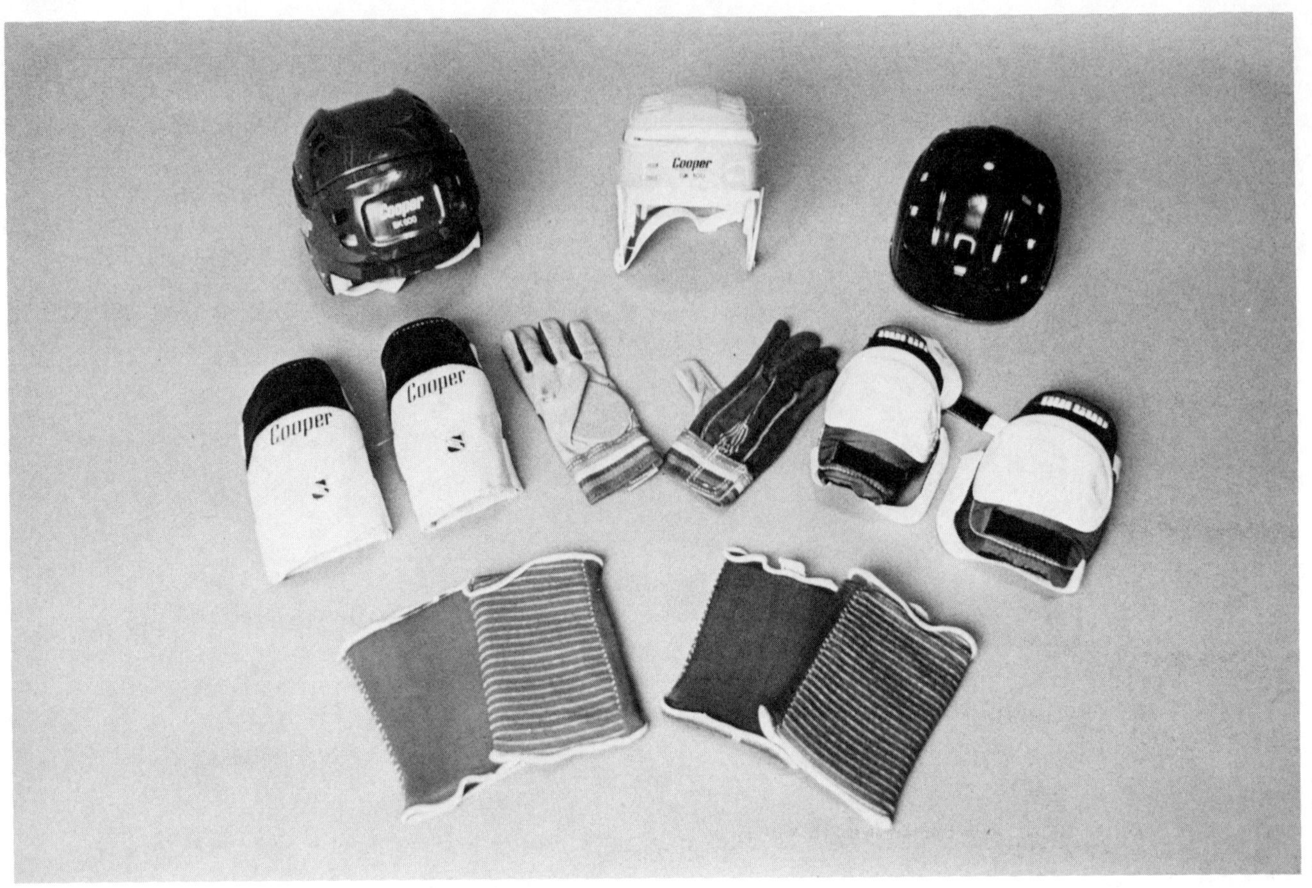

Cheapskates

Don't forget safety equipment.

wheels and trucks on *any* firm pair of leather-soled boots—from Frye boots to cowboy boots.

Choose a skate boot for *support* and *comfort*. And the higher the quality, the longer it will last.

THE TOE STOPS HERE

After you pick your wheels, you should find choosing toe stops a snap. (Inexpensive skates may not come with toe stops, but they are advised for safe skating.) They are essential for stopping and for performing many artistic and roller disco steps.

Toe stops vary in size and flexibility: The *harder* they are (polyurethane or plastic), the longer they'll last. The *larger* they are, the more protection—but the less maneuverability—they'll provide.

Toe-stop styles keep changing: You can choose from round or triangular toe stops, solid or grooved. Buy colored toe stops to match your wheels—from glistening white (that may soon become gray from use) to translucent yellow or Day-Glo pink.

SIDE ORDERS

Have your roller skates dyed any color under the sun, and buy fluffy pom-poms to match. From checkered laces to hand-painted boot-covers, from houndstooth knee socks to satin shorts, the wide choice of "roller rags" makes outfitting yourself for skating fun. But be sure to wear clothes that are *safe* for skating—with nothing dangling down to trip up your wheels.

Paul Boorstin

Snazzy T-shirts make the scene in the roller disco

Consider buying safety equipment: a plastic helmet, wrist guards, knee and elbow pads. And for those who don't have enough of the natural built-in variety, a "fanny pad" may be a good addition.

KEEPING THEM ROLLING: SKATE MAINTENANCE

Whatever skates you choose to buy, here are some simple rules to keep them in mint condition:

Before you put on your skates

1. Spin all four wheels on each skate, watching for wobbles and listening for creaks and squeaks.
2. Examine the lock-nuts on each wheel to assure they're holding the ball bearings in place.
3. Check to make certain that the main axle bolts (connecting the axles to the trucks and holding the rubber cushions in place) are tight. (You can adjust them to suit your needs, as discussed earlier. If they are too loose, the ride will be sloppy; if they are too tight, you'll find it more difficult to turn.)

Remember to:

1. Have the skate shop clean your ball bearings when the wheels begin to feel sticky or spin unevenly. Loose ball bearings get dirtier much more quickly than sealed bearings, but if you keep them clean, even the loose bearings will wear a long, long time.
2. Rotate the wheels on your skates just as you would the wheels on a car—once or twice a year, depending on how often you skate.
3. Skates aren't mukluks. Avoid skating through water, sand, dirt, or mud, to ensure the longevity of your wheels and bearings.

Chapter 3

Roll 'Em: Take

Skating Starters: Begin with the Basics

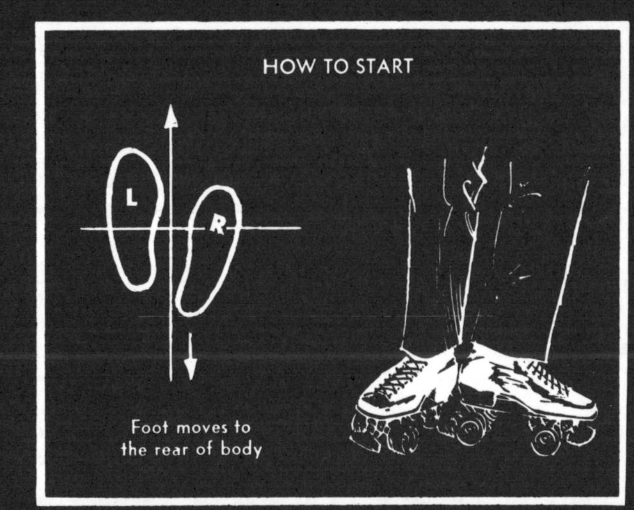

RSROA

GETTING THE WHEELS ROLLING

Learning to roller-skate is like learning to walk—only harder—for skating requires better balance and coordination. Actually, skating is more like *sliding* than walking, and getting the knack of moving on wheels can be as precarious, at first, as a stroll down an icy sidewalk. On skates, you must first grow accustomed to the friction between you and the ground, and gain control over your rolling movement. But once you master the simple basics—forward and backward gliding, stopping, and turning—you'll be able to move on wheels with freedom and grace.

WHEELING INSTEAD OF WALKING

Lace up your skates and cautiously try out your new relationship to the ground. Lean forward, and you'll roll forward; lean backward, and your wheels will roll backward, in the direction your body weight dictates. If you begin *walking* on skates, your body will pitch forward, sending your rear skate sliding out behind you.

To skate correctly, imagine that one skate is the carrier of your body, propelled forward by a slight push from your opposite foot against the ground. Hold the *pushing skate* on the ground with enough body weight to ensure the longest possible push.

TAKING OFF

1. Begin with feet close together, forming a V, right foot slightly ahead of the left. Shift your weight over the *pushing skate* (left foot in the diagram) and begin the push out to the side and back, using pressure on the inside front of the pushing skate. This propels the *carrying skate* (right foot in diagram) forward.
2. Hold pushing skate on the surface until your knee straightens and pushing leg lifts off the floor (don't kick it back), and lifts to a 40-degree angle behind you. (The pushing skate is called the *free leg* once it is off the ground.)
3. Keep *carrying leg* slightly bent. When you begin to lose momentum at the end of a comfortable distance, return the *free leg* to the ground, rebending the knee, and push off with it to repeat the whole process—rolling now on the left foot.

The harder you push off, the longer and faster you'll roll forward. The smoother you follow through (lifting the free leg off the ground), the smoother your glide forward.

SKATING BALANCE AND POSTURE

Balancing while skating is different from balancing while walking. When you walk, one leg always goes out ahead of the body. It is the opposite in skating. The leg that is off the

Taking Off

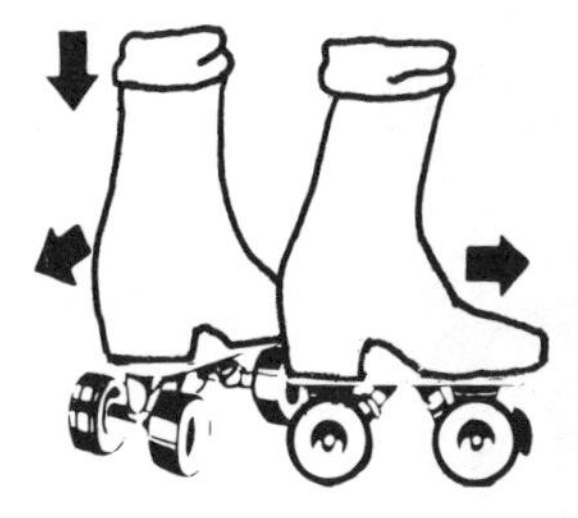

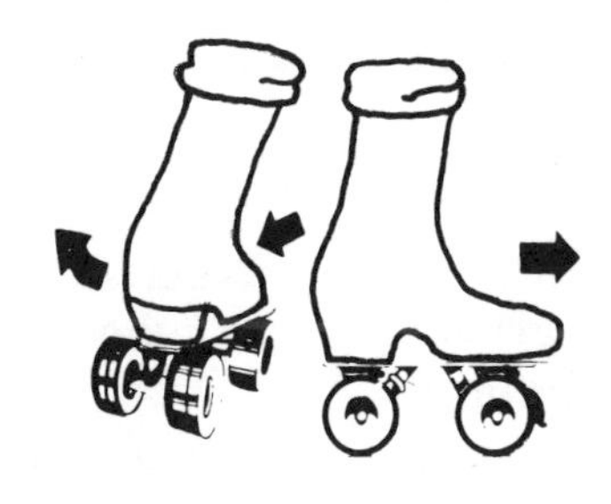

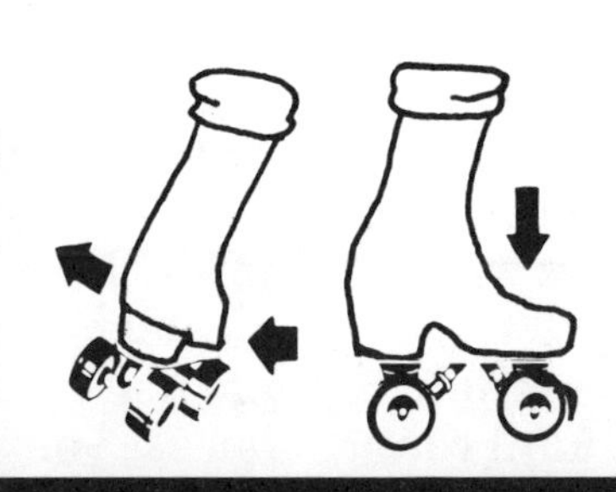

Sharon Boorstin

Incorrect body lean.

skating floor (the *free leg*), goes behind your body to provide propulsion for the carrying skate, and helps you maintain your balance.

Balance weight directly over the middle or *ball* of the *carrying* foot, rather than the heel. Body should be erect and supported by a firm back. Keep head up, eyes looking straight ahead.

BODY LEAN— CONTROLLING YOUR AIM

Practice pushing off and rolling straight ahead on left foot and then the right, until you feel confident balancing on one foot at a time. Next: how do you control your direction? How do you get where you want to go?

A roller skate has no tiller or steering wheel. But the rubber cushions between the boot and the wheels (in the "truck") allow you to aim your direction by shifting your weight to rock the skate from side to side. The skate will follow every movement of this *body lean.*

Lean to the *outside* or *inside* of the skate you are using (the *carrying skate*), never forward or to the rear. Transmit pressure to the *carrying skate* with your *entire* body. Keep upper body firm and straight, hips and shoulders in line. Don't bend from the waist, and don't lead with your head or arms. When you use your *whole* body to aim your direction, very little lean will be required to curve.

Correct body lean.

Sharon Boorstin

The Toe-Stop Stop

RSROA

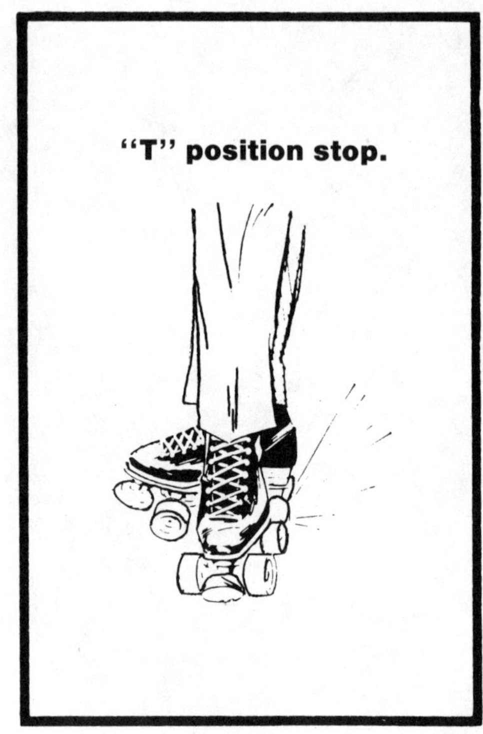
"T" position stop.

RSROA

STOPPING

Once you can skate forward and control your aim, you must learn how to stop. (Watch your step at first, for your body will be obeying Newton's laws of motion!) There are several methods for stopping, some trickier than others:

For Beginners—The Toe-Stop Stop

Simple: As you are skating forward, lower the free leg, toe pointed down toward the ground behind the skating foot, and exert pressure with the rubber toe stop against the ground until you gradually slow down and come to a halt.

The "T" Position Stop

Practice this first while standing still, and then from an increasingly faster roll. Try to resist lunging forward while you're stopping; support your body with a firm back and lean very slightly against your direction of travel until skates come to a halt.

1. With right skate placed behind heel of left skate, form a "T" position (see diagram). Keep body upright, knees bent, and push off onto left skate.
2. Gradually lower right skate back to "T" position, pressing middle of skate into heel of left skate.
3. Slowly transfer body weight to right skate. The friction of the right skate on the skating surface will act as a brake, since the wheels cannot now roll.

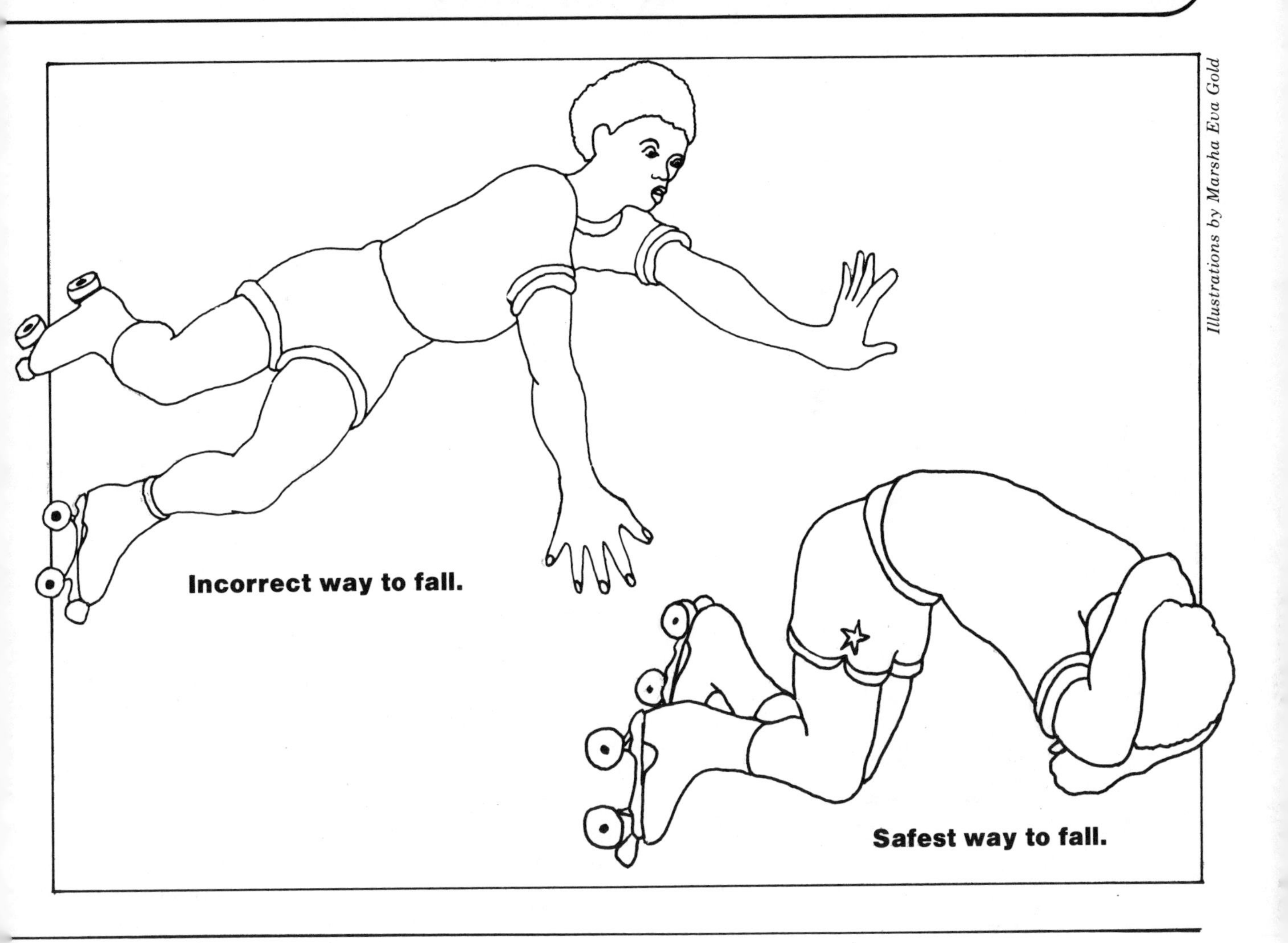

FALLING

It's no joke: the ground is the hardest thing about skating. And the taller you are, the more you'll have to learn to live with it when the inevitable laws of gravity catch up with you. Children can find falling fun—it's a short way down. But when an adult sees it coming, he or she should prepare to meet the earth in a way that will soften the blow.

A natural reaction when you start to fall might be to put out an arm to brace yourself, but if you do, you may end up with that arm in a cast! Your body can best absorb shock if it is *loose*. When you begin to topple, bend your knees rapidly and "fold in" your body, so that you get close to the ground as you go down in one *thump*, without arms or legs sticking out to suffer the full impact.

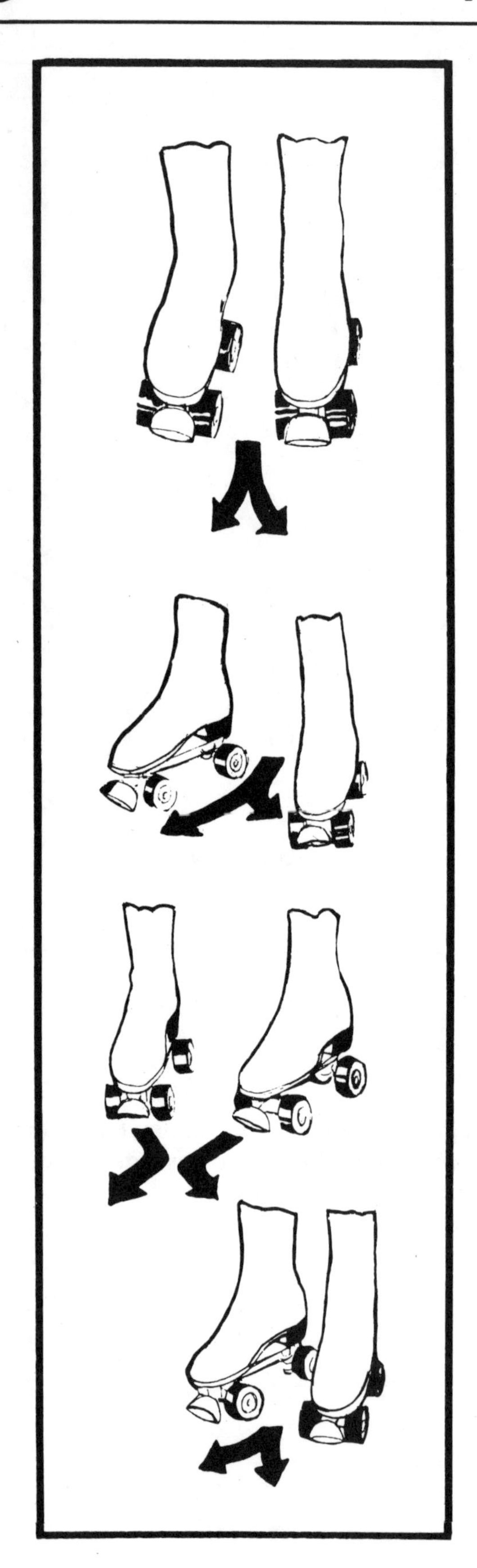

Scissors movement forward.

THE SCISSORS SKATING STEP—A SKATING TECHNIQUE AND EXERCISE

The scissors stroke is one of the first steps a beginning skater can master to gain a sense of confidence, for in this maneuver, the skates never leave the ground. In addition, exerting pressure against the ground as you build up momentum strengthens the inner thigh muscles, calves, and ankles.

1. Keeping posture erect, bend both knees.
2. Heels together, toes angled 45 degrees apart, exert side pressure on inside of each skate and force feet apart to a distance approximately shoulder-width.
3. Exert pressure on inside of skates, turning toes inward, pigeon-toed, and pull skates back together until they are approximately two inches apart.
4. Repeat this action, out and in, in a slow but continuous movement. Skate around the rink several times in this "scissors" step, using all muscles in the lower half of your body.

BACKWARDS SKATING

Skating backwards *seems* difficult because you can't see where you're going. But it really isn't—if you use the same principles of balance and movement as in forward skating. Learn to skate backwards by practicing the

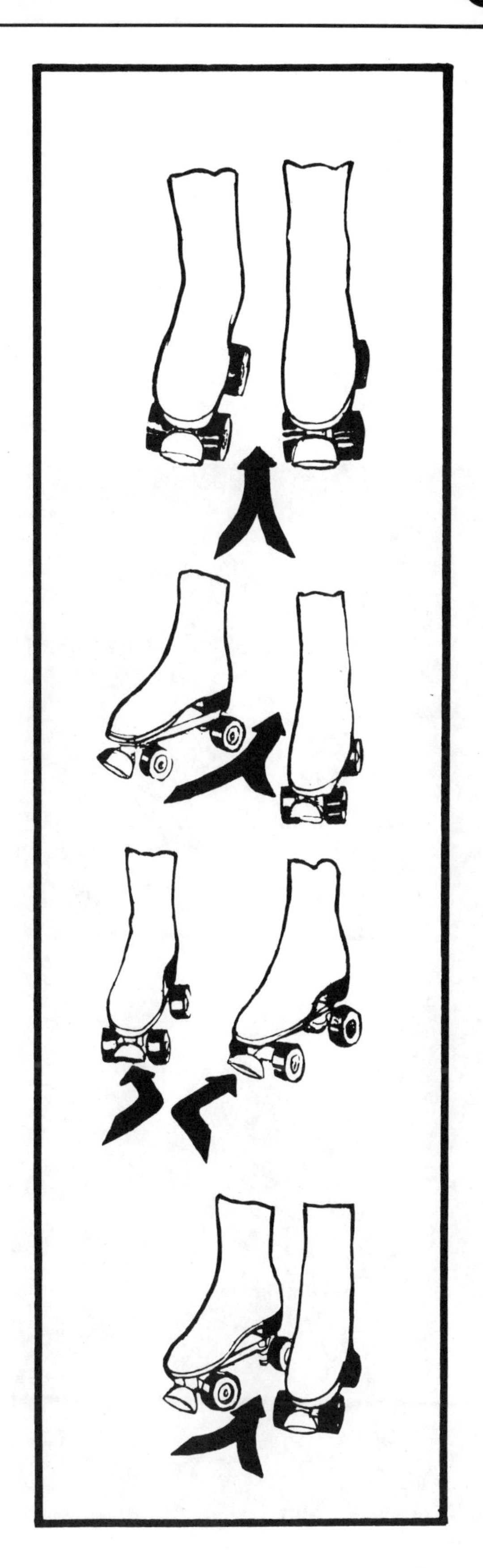

Backward scissors movement.

backwards scissors movement.

Backwards Scissors Skating

1. Stand with back straight, weight balanced over balls of your feet. Flex knees moderately, assuming a close-together, slightly pigeon-toed position.
2. Exerting pressure on inside wheels of both skates, push the two skates apart—no more than twelve inches. (Practice this first by pushing yourself away from a wall or rail, or by having someone hold your hands and push you backwards as he or she skates forward.)
3. When skates are apart, begin pulling skates back together, heels pointing inward. Keep pressure on inside of your skates throughout.
4. Secrets of success: don't let feet move more than twelve inches apart, and don't let heels touch as you pull skates back in from the outside position (or you'll end up in a dead halt).

Backwards Skating

When you feel comfortable skating the "backwards scissors," and you're not teetering, or worrying about what you'll slam into (do peek over your shoulder!), you should be ready to try skating backwards.

Begin with the "backwards scissors" to build up momentum, then lift each skate alternately off the skating surface, using the stroke-and-glide motion of forward skating, only in the opposite direction. Point free skate

Spread Eagle

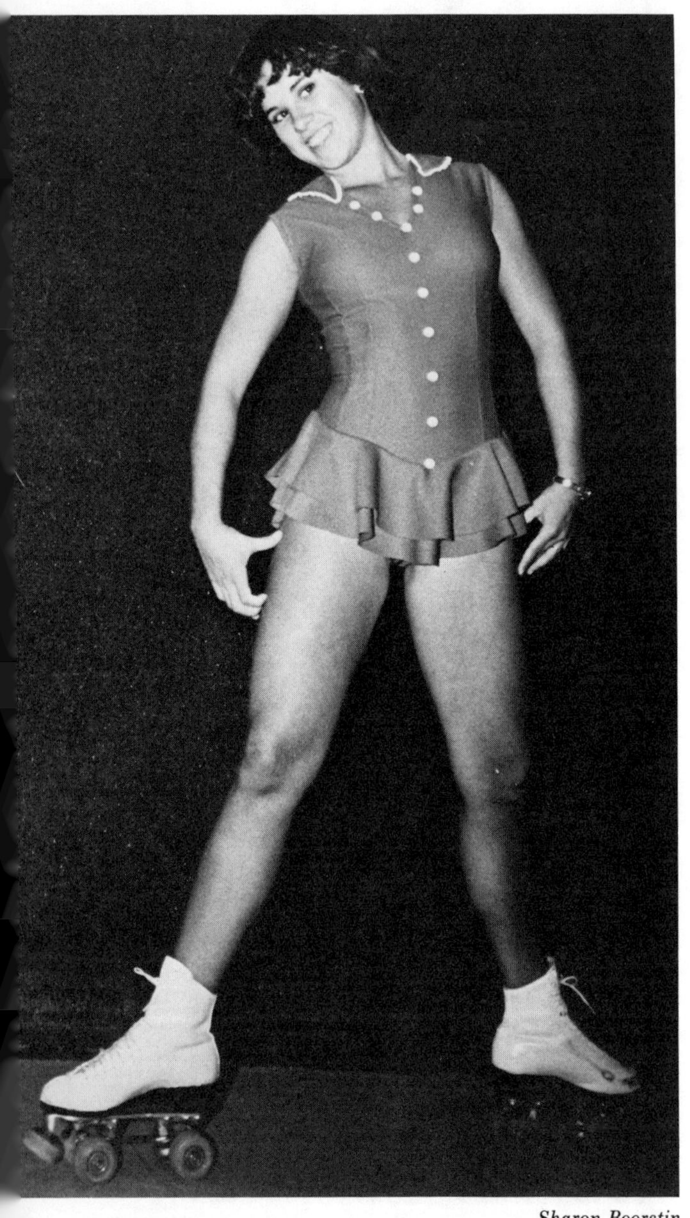

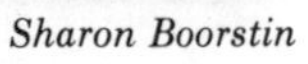

Sharon Boorstin

Sharon Boorstin

in front of the body, low off the ground. Lower free foot and push off once again with other foot when you begin to slow down.

A Simple Backwards Skating Stop
When skating backwards, the easiest way to stop is to lean forward and rise up onto your toe stops. (Don't try this while skating forward, or you may pitch forward onto your face!)

SPREAD EAGLE

This sideways-moving skating technique is easy for a beginner to master—and it *looks* good. You can add flair by changing the arm positions.

With heels close together, toes pointed in opposite directions, travel in a circle, one foot leading forward, the other trailing backward.

Vary the "spread eagle" by varying arm positions and by spreading legs wider apart.

Surf-Side Position
A variation of the "spread eagle" ideal for skating on the curved surfaces of a skateboard park: legs apart, *knees bent,* toes pointed outward. (See Chapter XI.)

Mohawk, Spread Eagle, or Two Turn

Sharon Boorstin

THE MOHAWK, SPREAD EAGLE. OR TWO TURN

When you can skate forward and backward with ease and have mastered the "spread eagle," you can learn to *turn* from a forward to a backward, or a backward to a forward, skating position.

1. Traveling forward in a straight line, shift

Mohawk, Spread Eagle, or Two Turn

Sharon Boorstin

Sharon Boorstin

weight onto right foot. Rotate left free leg and drop the backwards-aiming left skate onto the skating surface, close by the heel of right skate, toe pointing in opposite direction of right, forward-traveling skate. (This is the "spread eagle" position.)

2. Immediately lift right skate from floor, rotate it, and drop it down on skating surface alongside left skate, so that you are traveling backward.

Reverse procedure to turn from backward skating position to forward skating position.

RSROA

ONE FOOT, OR THREE TURN

The "three turn" may look harder, but it is as easy as the "two turn," and once you get the hang of it, you can escalate it into a "jump turn."

Essential to success in the "three turn": erect posture, firm positioning of the body over the skates, and a good push-off onto the carrying skate. Your body will rotate above the carrying skate in the direction of the turn.

1. Traveling forward on right foot, transfer weight to front wheels.
2. Using the elasticity of your wound-up body, with your free leg firm and behind your body, pivot around on front wheels of right skate, sliding rear wheels around in contact with floor. (You're now skating backwards.)
3. Secret is to keep weight on front wheels until turn is completed. Extend arms to maintain balance. *Don't kick* into turn with free leg.

WALTZ OR JUMP TURN

In this dramatic turn, your free leg kicks up and around, lifting your body off the ground as you turn from one skating direction to the other.

1. Push off with right foot, knees bent. Shift weight to left foot. Balance with arms, lean forward, and go up onto left toe stop.
2. Swing right arm around, right foot in air, twisting body around following right arm.

3. Pull arms and body up, still swinging around, leading with right arm and right leg, and bring left foot *totally* off the ground.
4. As you swing around, facing opposite direction, bring right foot down first, knees bent, arms up for balance.
5. Shift weight onto left foot, arms down, knees bent, and glide off on left foot.

Chapter 4

Skating for Your

Rolling into Good Shape

Life

RSROA

"Skating sends the blood to the surface of the body in healthy circulation, and by rousing the dormant functions of the skin, relieves the overworked internal organs and gives new life and vigor to the general system."

(Henley's Manual of Roller Skating, 1885)

No one will argue: roller-skating is as healthy for skaters in the 1970s as it was for our great-grandparents. The push and stroke movement involved in skating strengthens arm, leg, and back muscles, and as you build up momentum, the cardiovascular system works harder, with lasting benefits for the entire body.

Other activities do the same thing, of course—jogging, swimming, bicycle-riding. But undoubtedly, roller-skating is one of the most sociable and enjoyable. And since you must exercise for good health, why not have fun doing it?

SKATING OFF POUNDS

You'll never find a fat roller-skating champ. Or even a plump silver medalist. Competitive roller skaters who practice the two to three hours a day it takes to prepare for a meet can't help but shed extra pounds as they sharpen their skills for the big event. But you don't have to be that dedicated to lose weight with roller-skating. Normal roller-skating burns up *six calories a minute*—that's *360 calories an hour.* (Compare that to five calories a minute for swimming or cycling.)

Obviously, skating *alone* won't bring about weight reduction miracles. But skating *regularly*—while *eating moderately*—can't but help you lose weight.

How can you make skating work even more for you?

- *Increase your speed*—that's the first step. The faster you go, the harder your body will work, and the more calories you'll burn.
- *Then, increase your skating time.* A two-hour skating session can burn up *520 calories.* (That's equal to a good-sized cheeseburger!) If you're skating outdoors, venture *far far* away from your starting point, so that you'll *have* to cover that same distance to get back to home base. If you're skating at a rink, cut the coffee breaks to five-minute rest stops—and keep on rollin'.

As with many enjoyable forms of exercise, the fact that roller-skating is habit-forming only works to your advantage. If you'd rather skate than eat, using your feet can take the place of using your jaws. And even if you work up an appetite from all your exertion, a normal meal following skating will only replace the calories you just burned off, instead of allowing them to settle around your hips.

Here are some additional tricks that can help roller-skating help you reduce:

- Take a lesson yourself while your kids are taking theirs, instead of waiting for them on the sidelines with Coke and doughnut in hand.
- Go to the rink on Saturday night—or to

the park on Sunday afternoon—instead of lounging in front of the television, munching corn chips.

- Get your bridge-playing pals—and yourself—off your behinds and into a skating exercise class.
- Instead of splurging on an over-priced dinner for two, save money and calories—and put new life in your romance—rocking at the roller disco with your mate.

SKATING TO GET IN SHAPE

"We should skate as we eat, sleep, or tell the truth, just for the utility and the improvement it will individually produce. Skating unites the body and the mind more intimately than walking or running, with less fatigue for a similar amount of effort."

(Dr. T.L. Brown, June 1885)

Insightful advice, as true today as it was nearly a hundred years ago. For medical experts know conclusively now that being *out of shape* can be the cause of a lot of problems. In addition to causing the flabby muscles, potbelly, and the spongy layer around the midriff you can squeeze between thumb and forefinger, being unfit can also be the reason why you feel exhausted all the time, or find it hard getting up in the morning or staying up past ten o'clock at night. The fact that you're out of shape may be the reason why you find yourself puffing for breath after the slightest exertion—or why you can't always think clearly, or feel depressed. And not only do these nagging symptoms of being unfit make each day harder to live—and make *you* harder to live with—they can mean that you're actually shortening your life.

What Is Fitness?

Physiologists categorize physical fitness three ways: muscular, skeletal, and cardiovascular. *Muscular fitness* concerns the tone and strength of your muscles—which is promoted by exercise. *Skeletal fitness* describes your body's flexibility. Stretching develops skeletal fitness. The third kind of fitness, *cardiovascular*, refers to the strength and health of your heart and blood vessels—the fitness most important to your overall health.

As an activity that uses *all* your muscles, keeps you stretching and moving, roller-skating helps promote both muscular and skeletal fitness. And because roller-skating demands extra exertion from your heart and lungs, it fosters cardiovascular fitness—and general good health.

Fitness News You Can Use

Roller-skating turned up a winner when the President's Council on Physical Fitness asked seven medical experts to evaluate the healthful attributes of 14 sports. Each of the physicians judged the activities based on vigorous exercise for 30 minutes to an hour, four times a week. Then they rated them on a scale of 0 to 3, in terms of their effect on stamina, muscular endurance and strength,

	Physical Fitness				General Well-Being					
	Stamina	Muscular Endurance	Muscular Strength	Flexibility	Balance	Weight Control	Muscle Definition	Digestion	Sleep	**Total Score**
Jogging	21	20	17	9	17	21	14	13	16	**148**
Bicycling	19	18	66	9	18	20	15	12	15	**142**
Swimming	21	20	14	15	12	15	14	13	16	**140**
Skating (ice or roller)	18	17	15	13	20	17	14	11	15	**140**
Handball/Squash	19	18	15	16	17	19	11	13	12	**140**
Skiing—Cross Country	19	19	15	14	16	17	12	12	15	**139**
Skiing—Downhill	16	18	15	14	21	15	14	9	12	**134**
Basketball	19	17	15	13	16	19	13	10	12	**134**
Tennis	16	16	14	14	16	16	13	12	11	**128**
Calisthenics	10	13	16	19	15	12	18	11	12	**126**
Walking	13	14	11	7	8	13	11	11	14	**102**
Golf	8	8	9	8	8	6	6	7	6	**66**
Softball	6	8	7	9	7	7	5	8	7	**64**
Bowling	5	5	5	7	6	5	5	7	6	**51**

flexibility, balance, weight control, and other measures of well-being. When all the results were in, roller-skating came in *third*, beaten only by jogging and bicycling.

See for yourself: the scoreboard as tabulated in *Resident and Staff Physician* and reprinted in *U.S. News and World Report*, April 4, 1977.

Aerobics

Dr. Kenneth Cooper's revolutionary Aerobic Physical Fitness program is one of the most popular and successful of recent plans for getting people into good shape. And roller-skating can play an important part in it.

Aerobics ("with air") are exercises which demand oxygen, but which you can continue for long periods without running out of breath. The main objective of the aerobic plan is to *increase the amount of oxygen* that the body can process within a given time. This is called *Aerobic Capacity*. Jogging, swimming, cycling—and roller-skating—can all do this.

As you build up your performance in these

aerobic activities, your lungs gradually process more air with less effort, and your heart becomes stronger, pumping more blood with fewer strokes. If you do aerobics regularly, your ability to endure them longer increases each time, because as you increase your oxygen consumption, more oxygen is delivered to the muscles where it is converted into energy. After a while, doing aerobics begins to *energize* rather than *exhaust* you.

The Aerobic Plan, Roller-Skating, and You

Individuals following Dr. Cooper's plan set up an exercise schedule based on a set of charts which consider age, sex, and physical ability. Each week, they steadily increase their distance and speed in the aerobic activities, building strength and endurance. The goal is to gradually work up to earning *30 points* a week for maximum continued physical fitness.

Running a mile in eight minutes earns five points on Dr. Cooper's aerobic scale. Moderately vigorous roller-skating for one hour earns four points. True, jogging may be the most efficient way to earn points. But Dr. Max Novich, an orthopedic specialist and physician for the United States Olympics team, sees an advantage of skating over jogging for those just starting on a fitness program: "With medical authority, I can tell you that roller-skating encompasses the same benefits as jogging but with less effort. Running takes a lot of effort. It takes longer through roller-skating to accomplish the same thing that running does, but for people who haven't used their muscles, roller-skating is better."

In addition, it is possible to equal the benefits of jogging with roller-skating by increasing your skating rate. In 1972, Dr. Kenneth Rose, Chairman of the Committee on Exercise and Physical Fitness of the American Medical Association, conducted an extensive test on roller skaters and concluded that to obtain benefits to the cardiovascular system while skating, comparable to those from jogging, the average skater should approach a speed of one mile in six minutes and maintain this speed for at least twelve minutes.

We aren't advising that you give up jogging for roller-skating, but we do suggest that roller-skating is an excellent method for earning points in an overall fitness program. Roller-skating is a less rigorous, more social activity, certainly, than jogging. And even Dr. Cooper himself, in fact, encourages mixing a variety of aerobic sports when following his plan, to relieve the monotony of repetition. Remember, the goal is 30 points a week—earned any way you choose—for staying in good shape through aerobics.

STRICTLY FOR THE LADIES

"As a fashionable exercise for ladies, there is nothing so well adapted to the development and

Skating helps develop poise, while it works wonders on your figure.

display of a fine figure as roller skating; and in no way can a lady present equal elegance and grace as when circling about on skates. The accomplishment is becoming a very important part of every young lady's education."
(Ladies' Boudoir Magazine, 1855)

They knew back then what we still know today: skating develops poise and grace. What they *didn't* discover in the Victorian age, when skating dresses reached nearly to the floor, is that skates can work miracles on a lady's legs—both by firming them up and slimming them down, and by adding new height that makes them look as long and graceful as a beauty queen's.

Sharon Boorstin

There are hidden benefits for women who skate:

- During the menstrual cycle, stretching through skating is a guaranteed method for relieving menstrual cramps.
- The scissors skating step is not only good exercise for the thighs and buttocks, but it strengthens the vaginal walls as well.
- Roller-skating can provide emotional benefits. Work off tensions while gliding along. Use it to clear the cobwebs out of your head and replace them with fresh thoughts.
- Skating is one sport you can share with the whole family. Get to know your kids better by skating *with* them, instead of merely dropping them off at the rink. Learn to dance-skate with your husband. The family that skates together...

Sharon Boorstin

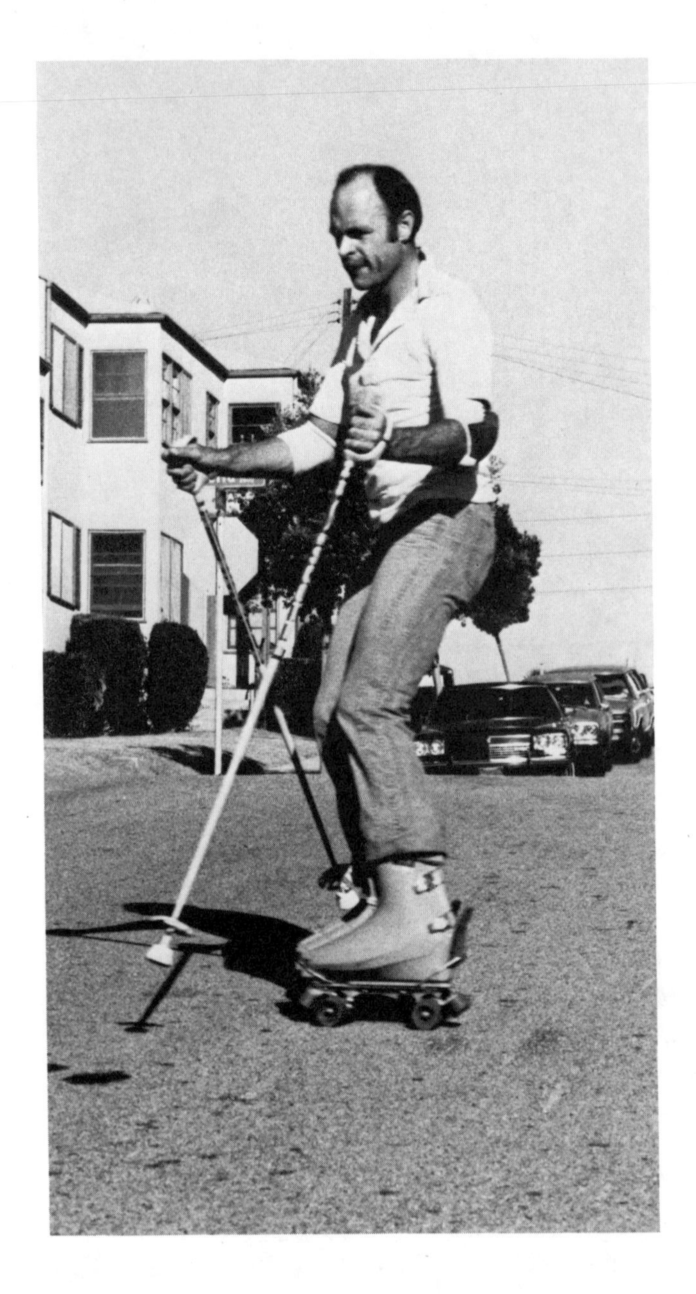

Ski skates make it possible to practice your christies on a concrete run.

SKATING FOR SKIERS

Whether you're a cross-country skier or a downhill racer, long before the snow falls, make a habit of working out *regularly* on roller skates. Roller-skating uses the same crucial leg muscles that you count on to help you get down the slope in one piece. Roller-

skating often—building up your time and speed—and doing the exercises in the chapter that follows, will help make your first foray onto the slopes enjoyable and painless.

Ski Skates

Now, you can even buy—or rent at the ski shop—*ski skates* that make it possible to practice your christies on a concrete run. The ski skate was the ingenious invention of a frustrated skier, Steve Parfet of Santa Monica, California, who was aching to get ready for the slopes while whiling away sunny days in Southern California's perpetual summer. Steve designed a pair of skates that would clamp right onto his ski boots, and Sure Grip skate company agreed to go with them.

Just slip the boot onto a metal plate only a little longer than the boot itself, which is mounted on soft urethane, precision-bearing wheels. A safety strap attaches the boot loosely to the skate, to keep it from rolling down the hill should it come off in a spill. With toe stops at the back as well as at the front of the skates, you can stop by leaning backwards if you get going too fast. Rubber pads come with the ski skates, to put onto the tips of your ski poles, so that you can use them on concrete.

Ski skates make it possible to work on parallel turns, and they are especially helpful for beginners first learning coordination on skis. Try them on a *gentle* hill. They're not designed for high-speed schussing—your neighborhood street offers no soft snow to cushion a fall.

IT REALLY WORKS

Brad and Mary Ann Swirnoff of West Los Angeles are proof positive that roller-skating can get you in shape. Thirty-three-year-old Brad, a writer and film director, was always "about to start jogging." Mary Ann, a mother and screenwriter, also 33, had been in and out of health spa exercise classes. But neither of them had been able to stick to any regular exercise regimen. When their blonde eight-year-old daughter, Jessica, wanted to show them the roller-skating skills she had learned in her school's PE program, she dragged them to Venice, expecting them to sit and watch her skate along the boardwalk. But when she saw all the other "grown-ups" on wheels, she insisted her parents rent roller skates, too, and to everyone's surprise, Mary Ann and Brad had a wonderful time.

After that, the Swirnoffs skated along the Venice boardwalk on Sundays. They relished the fresh ocean breezes, the colorful crowds, and the chance to enjoy a sport *en famille.* Soon they were finding excuses to skate there several times a week, after a dip in the ocean, while admiring the sunset. Before they knew it, they could roll the entire six miles from the skate rental shop to the Santa Monica pier and back, without feeling out of breath. They were hooked.

When Jessica bought them roller skates for Christmas, the Swirnoffs' roller-skating turf expanded from the Venice boardwalk to

Swirnoff family *Paul Boorstin*

the tree-shaded sidewalks in their own neighborhood. Now they were skating three or more times a week—to exercise, to run errands, to have fun. They began to feel more energetic and to sleep more soundly than they had in years. Brad was even motivated to intersperse jogging with his roller-skating, and Mary Ann realized that though she was eating as much as she always had, her hips were two inches trimmer.

When ski season finally rolled around, the Swirnoffs discovered another dividend of roller-skating: from the first day they hit the slopes, thanks to their new endurance and stronger leg muscles, they both skied like pros and suffered none of the hangover aches and pains that had turned them off to skiing the season before.

Today, the Swirnoffs are confirmed skate-o-holics. They have even found a way to include their 150-pound Great Pyrenees in this favorite family activity. If you see a gigantic shaggy white dog pulling a little girl on roller skates along the boardwalk in Venice, her parents trailing along, it's the Swirnoffs out getting their exercise.

Chapter 5

Exerskating

The Ultimate Skating Exercise Plan

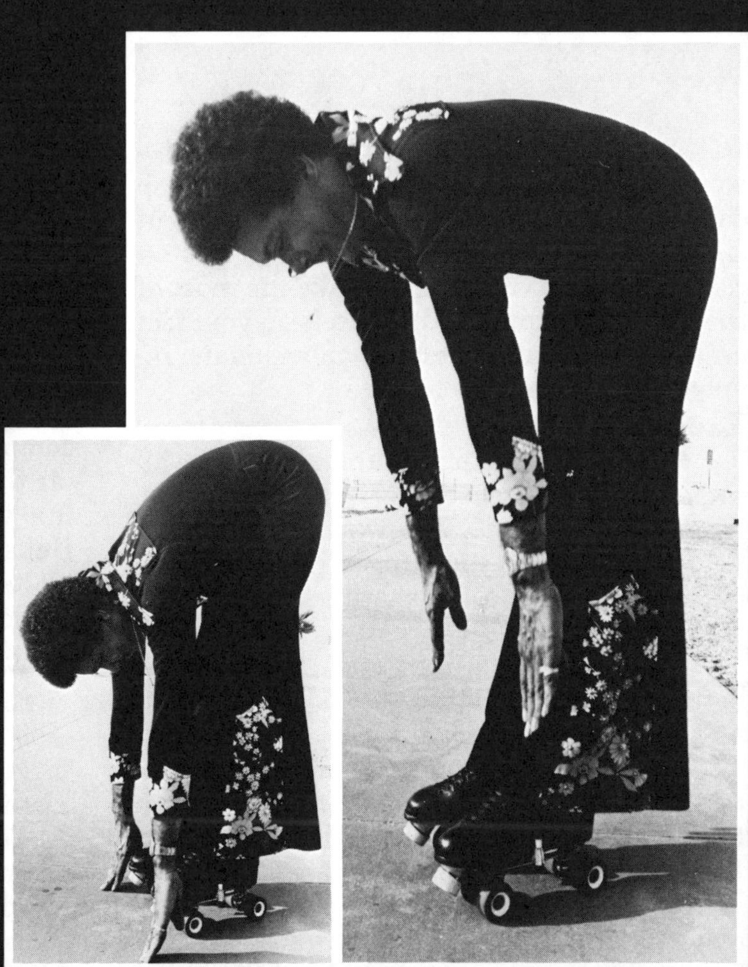

Sharon Boorstin

Of course, roller-skating by itself—traveling along at a normal clip—will burn up calories (360 an hour). But here is a series of simple exercises you can do while you're *on* roller skates, exercises that make the most of the five-plus pounds of the wheels on your feet and the natural stretching movements involved in skating.

Exerskating will:

- —Work on problem areas to slim away fat, and without developing bulging muscles, trim down legs, hips, and waist.
- —Limber you up, strengthen the muscles you use most in skating, and improve your endurance.
- —Help you attain attractive posture, better balance, and grace—on skates, and in all physical activities.

Put in ten to fifteen minutes of exerskating during your pleasure skating time—up front, or interspersed. Don't feel embarrassed. In fact, once you get into the swing of the more vigorous maneuvers, onlookers will undoubtedly try to imitate you, thinking you've invented some snazzy new roller tricks.

Above all, add exerskating exercises to your skating routine *gradually*, as your body is able to accommodate them. And *enjoy* them.

HOW TO AVOID ACHES AND PAINS

"Never skate until exhuasted. Exercise to be beneficial must always stop short of fatigue. If the limbs are so tired at night that you cannot sleep, then you have skated too much; or, if by tapping the muscles that are used most in skating you find they ache, then you have skated too much. This is a sure test, whether you have skated but three minutes or three hours."

(Henley's Manual of Roller Skating, 1885)

The hazards of roller-skating are nothing compared to the agonies of jogging. Runners jar their spines and knees—even risk flattening their feet—with every pounding stride. But skating can give you aching muscles and blistered toes, unless you follow this simple advice:

1. Wear thick, absorbent cotton socks that reach well above the tops of your skate boots.
2. Make sure skate boots fit properly. Lace them snugly (but don't cut off circulation). Test boots for flex and comfort. Do they rub you the wrong way? (Carry a couple of spare Band-Aids.) Do they support your ankles? (Press against the outside of your ankle—and then on the inside. The boots should provide support but still allow movement.) See that dangling shoelaces don't trip you up.
3. Warm up gradually for your skate. It's the first cold rush into the glide that causes later soreness. Be sure legs are stretched—arms, neck, and even toes limber.
4. Keep alert for muscle messages when you skate. If your leg starts to cramp, stop and give it a hardy massage. *Resting* should

mean more than flopping down on a bench: shake out legs, touch your toes. Take off your skates (or at least loosen the laces) for a while.

5. Lavish affection on your arms. Believe it or not, your arms work almost as hard as your legs when you skate. The faster you go, the more they pump to help propel you forward. Is your pinky ring suddenly tighter than usual? When you skate vigorously, the blood rushes to your fingertips. If your arms are tense and your fingers start to tingle, swing arms at shoulder level, touching fingers first in front of you and then in back. Shake them, marionette-style, shoulders loose. Try skating with hands on top of your head, sending the blood flowing away from your fingertips.
6. Sooner or later, the ground is bound to catch up with you. Relax if you begin to tumble, pulling arms close to your sides. (Don't extend an arm to brace your fall or it's likely to bear the full impact, when your body comes crashing down on top of it.) Once you're back on your feet, stop to shake out your limbs before taking off again.
7. Warming down *after* you skate is as important as warming up before. Flex your feet, touch your toes, and loosen shoulders before stepping back into your shoes.

WARMING UP

Hold on. Don't skate with a cold body. Take a few minutes to warm up and to get used to the added weight on the soles of your feet. Warm-ups get your juices flowing and limber up your muscles. They'll keep you from getting cramps, from falling because you're too stiff, and from aching the morning after.

Warm up on the carpet at the rink, or on the grass near the outside skating route—*not* where others may slam head-on into you.

For Starters

1. Shake out first one arm and then the other, keeping all joints soft, loosening elbows, wrists, and fingers.
2. Shake out one leg at a time, taking it more slowly at first, until you get used to the weight of the wheels. Hold on to some support so that you won't topple over.
3. Hunch and roll your shoulders; tighten, then let them drop. Push shoulders down as far as you can, then relax.
4. Arms at shoulder level, twisting only from the waist up, swing your torso to right and to left several times.
5. One arm over head, the other on your waist, do side stretches, first right hand up, then left hand up, bending over to each side and bouncing.
6. Loosen neck by circling it slowly, starting chin on chest; over against right shoulder, back as far as you can stretch, over against left shoulder, and relax.

Repeat these as many times as you need to—until you feel your muscles limbered.

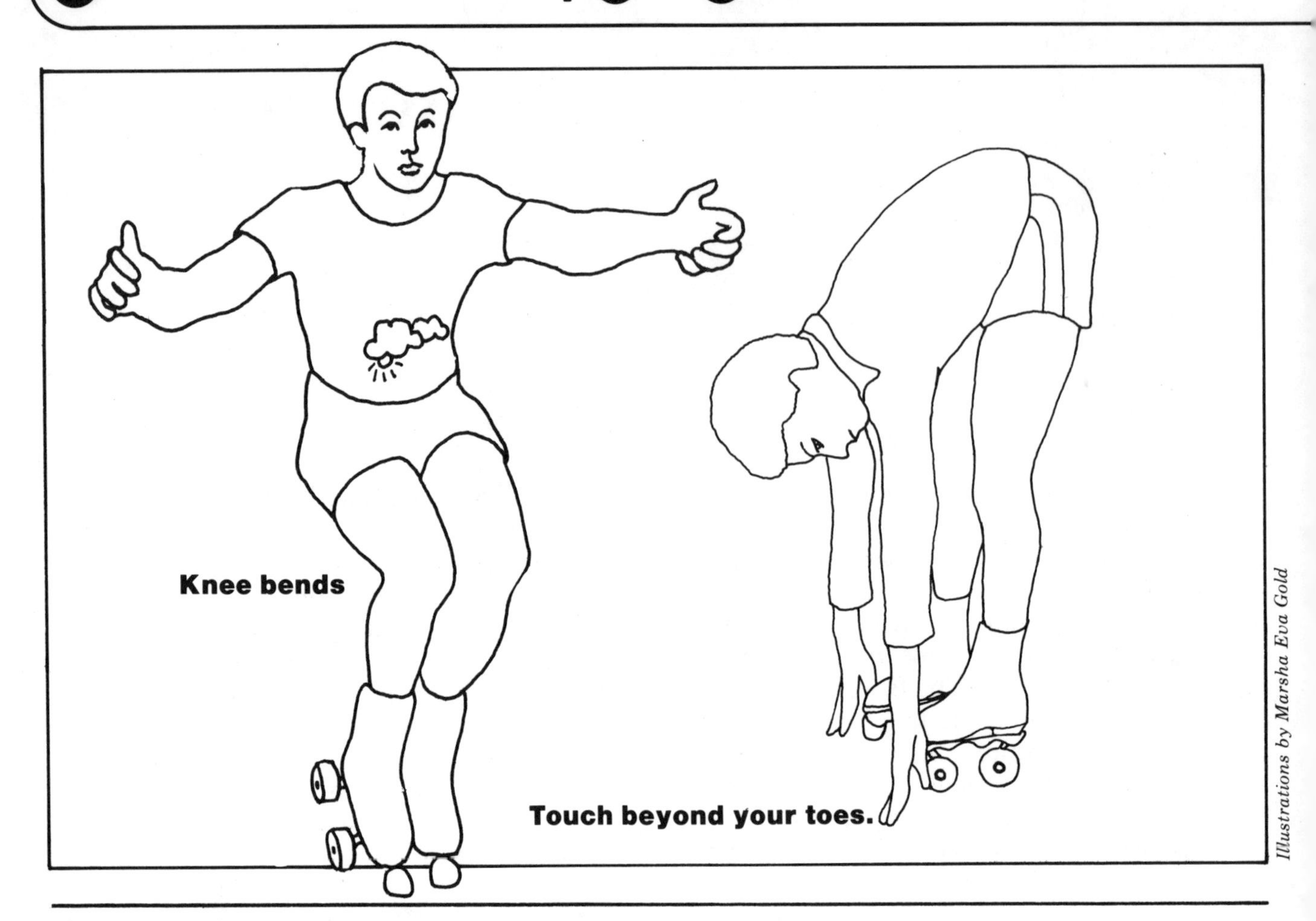

TOUCH BEYOND YOUR TOES

After you're loosened up, use the sudden new height from your high wheels to stretch out your legs. (But if you have any back problems, forget this one.) Begin gently, and don't strain. And don't expect to make it all the way the first time—but touching the *ground* should be your goal.

Heels together, form a V with your feet, toes pointed slightly out, so that your body won't slide backwards when you begin to bend forward. Keep legs straight, knees slightly soft. Lean forward from the waist, arms in front, head between them, reaching for the floor. Bounce gently, and then stretch to the ground. Continue to bounce, fingers pointed down. If you can graze the floor with your fingertips, you're a real pro.

Variation: To feel more muscle pull in your legs, do this same exercise with legs crossed, ankles locked together, first one leg in front, and then the other.

KNEE BENDS

This works on legs and waist, loosens knees, and helps your sense of balance. Hold on to some support at first, until you get the hang of it. Lean forward slightly and go up onto your *toe stops* and balance, then slowly bend your knees, back straight. Stay up on toe stops in the crouch position. Slowly straighten back up and repeat.

Variation: Do knee bends beginning in a spread eagle position—feet in a straight line, toes pointing out, legs apart. Go up onto toe stops and squat, then slowly straighten up. More difficult, but great for the thighs.

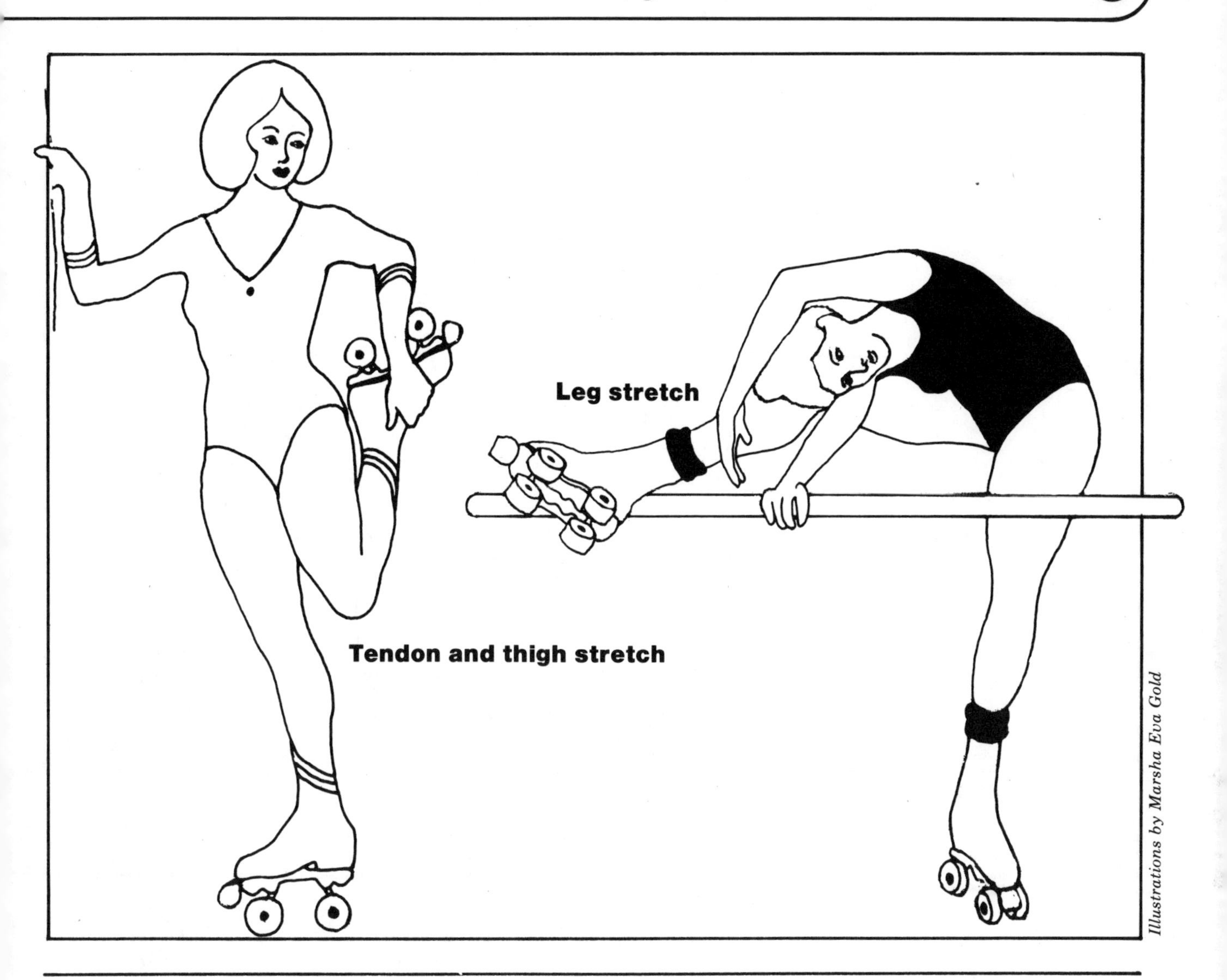

EXERSKATING AT THE RINK RAIL

1. Tendon and Thigh Stretch

This stretches the tendons at the back of the calves. Stand facing a wall or rail, and hold on with one hand. Slowly lift one foot in back, bending it from the knee, and holding it with your free hand, push the foot until the skate touches the back of your thigh (or is as close to it as you can get it.) Then slowly lower it back to the floor. Repeat this exercise several times, alternating legs, until leg muscles feel stretched out.

2. Leg Stretch

Stand facing a rail, or table that is slightly higher than waist level. Place right foot on the support, stretched out to the side, toe pointed. (Toes on supporting foot should be pointed out to the left.) Hold on to rail and stretch left arm up over your head. Bend over from the waist to the right, trying to touch your head to your right knee, then come up, back straight. Bounce five times, slowly, feeling the stretch in your side, back, waist, and legs. Change legs and repeat. Increase the number of bounces each time.

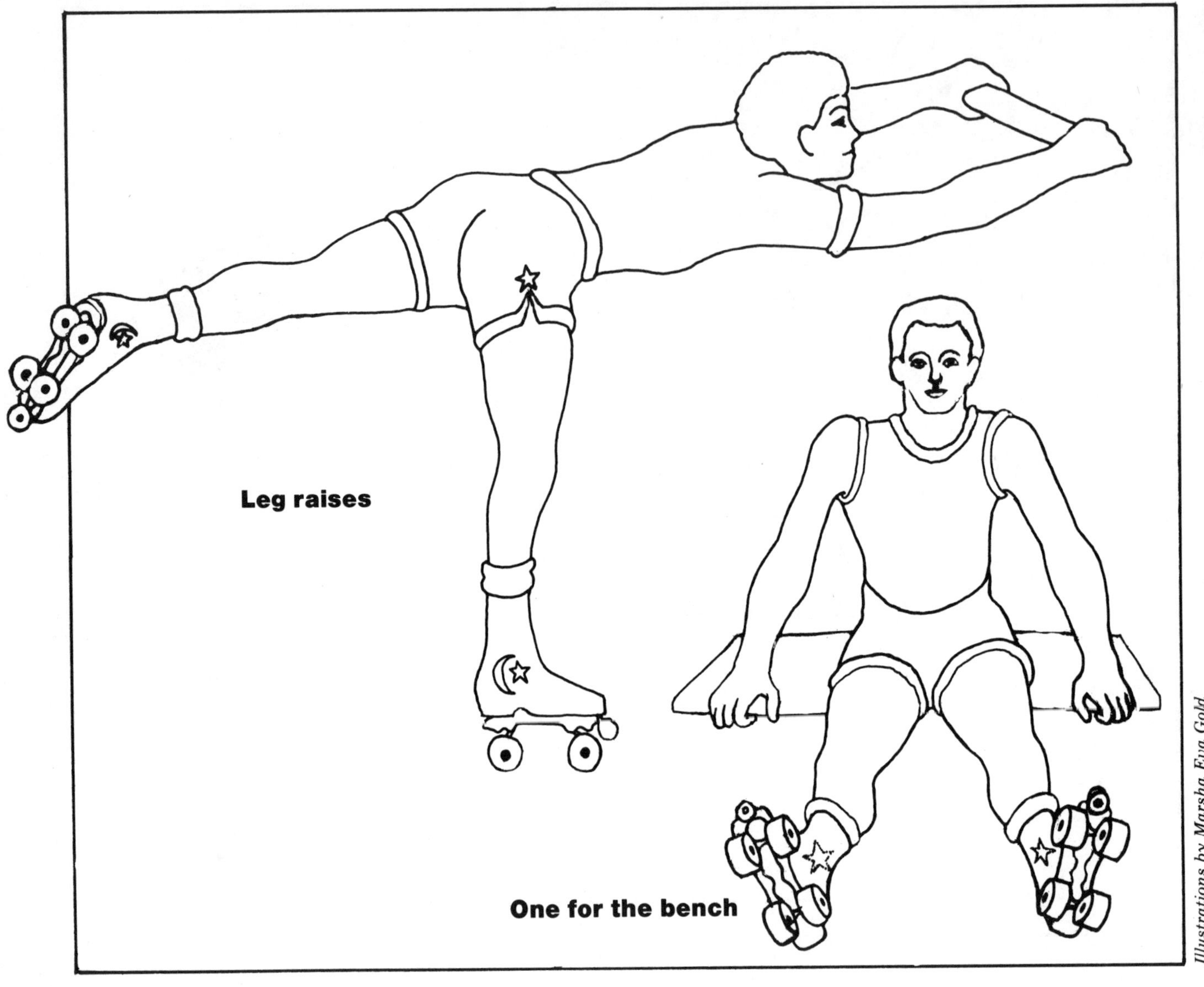

Illustrations by Marsha Eva Gold

3. Leg Raises

This strengthens leg muscles and works on waist and hips. Face rink rail and hold on with both hands. Roll backwards until arms and upper torso are parallel with the floor. Place feet together, legs straight, and very slowly, lift one leg straight behind you until it is in line with back and arms. Then lower it to the ground. Repeat this with other leg, ten times each. Keep head up, and increase speed with which you raise your legs. The extra exertion required to maintain a steady position without rolling helps, too.

4. One for the Bench

Here's one to do while you're resting on a bench. It can work wonders on stomach and thigh muscles. Sit forward, back straight, hands on the edge of the bench for support. Slowly raise legs until your feet are in a straight line out from your knees, then lower them, *slowly*, and repeat several times. Try not to swing legs up and down too suddenly.

EXERSKATING WHILE ROLLING ALONG

1. The Exaggerated Stroke and Kick
Accentuate every stroke and push as you skate. Set up your own concentrated rhythm, and put every ounce of energy into each stroke as you move, lifting free leg high behind you, toe very pointed, knee straight. Feel the increased tension in your leg and thigh muscles. A great way to tighten your buttocks.

Variation: Raise leg out to the side, in the same concentrated movement. Feel your inner thigh and hip muscles work.

2. Exaggerated Forward Lift
Skating slowly along, push off with right foot. Balancing on the left, raise right foot out *in front* of your body, toe pointed, leg straight, and hold it steady, parallel to the ground. (You may only be able to achieve a 45-degree angle at first.) Continue to hold leg steady as you glide, concentrating your energy on it, until you nearly stop rolling. Then lower it to the ground. Push off with left leg and repeat exercise with the left leg. This works on your thigh and stomach muscles.

Variation: Push off and raise your leg, as above, but instead of holding it steady, raise and lower it slowly from ankle to knee level, maintaining your balance until you stop rolling. Repeat with other leg. Feel the extra stretch this up-and-down movement gives.

Shooting the duck

Sharon Boorstin

3. Scissors Front and Back

Skate with the scissors stroke (explained in Chapter 3), but accentuate each movement, pressing your weight against the floor. The exertion required to keep you going without your feet leaving the surface builds up inner thighs and strengthens calves and ankles.

4. Shooting the Duck

This requires good balance and lots of practice, but it is challenging and fun, and it strengthens leg, hip, buttocks, and stomach muscles. Build up a steady momentum, skating in a straight line. Then bend over, touch toes, and squat down, knees bent, sitting back on heels. When you're balanced, use your hands to extend right leg out in front, and if you can, keep it out there *without* holding it up. Practice the same maneuver with the left leg.

Sharon Boorstin

5. Arm Positions

Create new arm positions while gliding forward in a straight line. Use the five arm positions of ballet: both out to the side; one raised in a curve over your head, the other in front, etc. Hold each arm position for one length of glide. Change arm positions as you change feet. Keep tummy in, head high. This easy exercise helps improve your balance while moving and remedies any incorrect pressure on the gliding foot. Invent new arm positions to try.

6. Taking the Rail Exercises Away from the Rail

Once you feel confident about your sense of balance, do the tendon stretch (bending knee, pressing skate up against thigh) and leg raises (bending over from waist until free leg and torso are parallel to the ground) while skating along in a slow, steady pace.

Chapter 6

Skating For You

From Tiny Tots to Senior Citizens

ng and Old

RSROA

TINY TOTS TAKE OFF

"If they can walk, they can skate," contends Jerry Nista, professional skater who has toured the country in exhibitions since 1950, and his two-year-old son, Brett Ashley, is already following in his father's skate steps. Owner of the Skate-o-Rama in Downey, California, and coach to many regional and national skating champions, Jerry Nista is an expert when it comes to roller-skating, and his convictions about the value it can have for children are supported by educators and medical men throughout the country.

It is no coincidence that the Boy Scouts of America have long offered a merit badge in roller-skating and that public schools across the United States use roller-skating in their regular physical education programs. Doctors often prescribe a regimen of roller-skating to correct pigeon toe and knock knee problems. When children skate, they are pressing on the outside edge of the skate every time they stroke, which helps turn the feet and knees out—approaching a normal walking position.

Roller-skating can be beneficial to children, beginning even at pre-school ages. Skating is challenging—but not impossible—for kids of that age to learn. It improves their coordination and sense of balance, and as they gain competence, they gain a greater sense of self-confidence. If they can walk, they can skate....

TEACHING TINY TOTS

For even the tiniest children, learning to skate can be an adventure. They're still close enough to the ground so that falling is part of their everyday experience—and no big deal—especially if the skating teacher makes it into a game. *Let the kids get a big bang out of falling.*

Wanting to skate is the first key to a child's ability to learn how. If the teacher is warm, cheerful, and encouraging, the child will want to imitate him. And if the little child sees bigger children having a good time skating, he won't take much convincing to join in.

1. Slow down the wheels on the tot's first pair of skates by tightening them with a wrench. Or put him on the inexpensive, plastic strap-on skates you can buy at the dime store. (They do not have ball bearings.)
2. First, the child must become accustomed to the added weight of wheels on his feet—and the added height.
3. Being able to *walk* with that extra weight and extra height takes some getting used to. Help him practice, holding on to the child's hand as long as he needs it for security and balance. And when he is ready to try moving on his own, let go—but stand by—and be prepared to make a game out of falling. (The tot's ego shouldn't be

A tiny tot learning to "shoot the duck" will feel proud of himself.

RSROA

Plastic strap-on skates without ball bearings are slow and safe for the first spin.

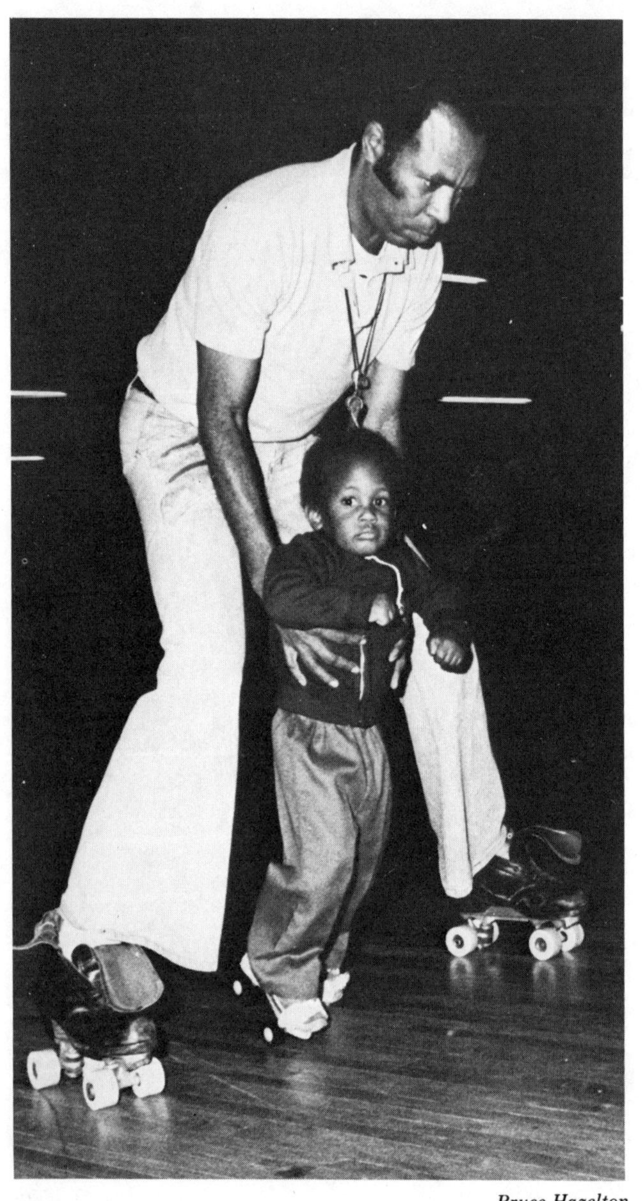

Bruce Hazelton

Kids can enjoy racing as soon as

hurt any more than his fanny.)

4. When the child feels comfortable, and can walk without your assistance, loosen the wheels. Guide him so that, both feet on the ground, he becomes accustomed to rolling forward on the wheels.
5. Next, help the child balance on one foot at a time—without rolling forward out of control. Lend a steadying hand when necessary.
6. Now, guide him so that he is rolling forward first on one foot alone, and then

RSROA

they feel comfortable on wheels.

Pro, Jerry Nista's two-year old son, Brett, gets a big bang out of falling.

Warren Pope

the other.

7. Show him how to push off with one foot and glide forward on the other. Hold his hand and help by pushing or pulling gently, until he can achieve some momentum on his own.

Once the tiny tot can stroke and glide, the rest is like teaching anyone at any age how to skate for the first time. The key to teaching little kids is to *make it fun and to minimize the gravity of the gravity situation.* Most importantly of all—*allow the tiny tot to progress at a pace most comfortable for him.*

Joe Frazier

James Roat

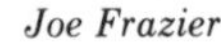

SKATING FOR SENIOR CITIZENS

News: At 86, C.J. Gerber is "Gramps" to the customers at the Holiday Roller Rink in Elkhart, Indiana. He's one of the regulars himself, taking a full load of dance, figure, and freestyle classes, and he even gives skating exhibitions with partners sometimes *60* years younger than he!

News: Evert McGill of Kansas City rides the bus to his favorite rink every Tuesday night. At 86, his elaborate tricks dazzle youngsters who have a hard time keeping up with him.

News: Every Saturday night, weather permitting, James Roat of Van Wert, Ohio, drove from his rural farm to Beyer's Roller Rink where he indulged in his favorite pastime—roller-skating. Lots of people do that.... So what? So... James Roat, 92, did it until he was 90 years old!

YOU'LL WEAR OUT BEFORE YOU'LL ROLL OUT

These vigorous oldsters prove an important truth: it is never too late to skate. Skating senior citizens are discovering—or practicing what they knew all along—that we can slow down the body's aging by keeping it going.

Lack of use is the real villain in old age: unused muscles grow flabby, hearts that are never challenged to pump blood falter. A proper dosage of exercise is good medicine—even life-saving. Too much at once might be harmful, but moderate exercise helps renew vitality and actually enables the body to withstand the unexpected extremes of stress that may befall it from time to time.

Skating for senior citizens is wise and healthful exercise. It's easy to master. You don't need any special athletic ability. You don't need to buy special equipment or sports outfits. You can do it at a leisurely pace, and you can stop and rest when you choose. It is an

(far left) Evert McGill, 86, does the "heel splits."

(opposite) James Roat didn't give up skating until he turned 90.

(this page) C.J. Gerber, 86, skates to keep young and often dance-skates in exhibitions.

C. J. Gerber

inexpensive recreation, and unlike more rigorous sports, such as football—and even singles tennis—skating is one that can be pursued safely long past retirement.

RULES FOR ROLLING AFTER 65

Once you learn how to swim, no matter how many years have passed since you've done it, if you get thrown into a lake, you'll remember how! Likewise with roller-skating. If it has been five—or 50—years since you skated, when you put on a pair of skates, twice around the rink and you'll remember how to do it.

Senior citizens can skate for health, for companionship, to keep alert, to achieve new poise, and to know the pride of being able to feel competent in a sport. But when skating after the age of 65, it's a good idea to follow these simple safety rules:

1. Check with the doctor before skating. Ask his recommendations about the amount of time you can safely put in—when you're just beginning, and later, after you're a real pro.
2. Wear comfortable clothes.
3. Do some gentle limbering-up exercises before putting your skates on and after they're laced up.
4. If it has been years since you last skated, or if you've never skated at all, take a lesson from a professional teacher.
5. Skate during a time at the rink or in the park when there are likely to be fewer people. (Avoid busy weekends.)
6. Find friends—old or young—to skate with. Half the fun of skating is sharing it with someone else.
7. Set your own pace. Don't try to outdo youngsters who can skate circles around you.
8. Gradually build up your skating speed and the amount of time you put in.
9. Make skating a habit. Do it several times a week. Like all forms of exercise, the benefits of skating come from regular exertion.

Chapter 7

United Skates of

A Look at Neighborhood Skating Centers

America

RSROA

Just off the 605 at Imperial Highway, in the freeway maze of Southern California, is Downey Skate-o-Rama, the quintessential skating paradise of the '70s. When you pull into the parking lot, the rink looks like any old roller barn you'd find by the side of the road in the '50s, but once you push through the swinging doors, you're in for a big surprise. At Skate-o-Rama, there is no organ music "da-da-da-dumming" in a drafty, hangar-sized room—no thunderous racket of wooden skate wheels on wooden floors assailing your eardrums. Instead, you enter a radiant park, where the theme color isn't the old washed-out beige of the rinks of bygone days, but *green*—green plush carpets, green papered walls, and the green of 16 life-sized weeping willow trees, their branches twinkling with lights and twittering with bird songs. The wall at the far end presents a skyline of green rolling hills to offset the skating floor—a silver-blue *pond* bordered by Astroturf and park benches. Friendly floor guards in park ranger uniforms rent you a pair of skates, and when the skating session begins, top forty tunes blast in over 60 speakers to send you sailing around the floor.

Skate-o-Rama is just one of the 4000 up-to-date skating rinks that dot the country and make roller-skating indoors today more than just circling a floor. The new rinks transport you to a fantasyland where you become part of the entertainment. The Coachlite in Kansas City features a European atmosphere, with custom-made coach lamps, wrought-iron tables and chairs in the snack area, and a wall-sized mural of the French Riviera near the rink floor. In Gresham, Oregon, a 95-foot painting of Mount Hood rises above the super-silent glistening ice-blue floor, making skaters feel as if they're skating in a winter wonderland. And Golden Skate, in the gold rush country of Ramon, California, is decked out like an Old West town, where customers buy tickets at an old-fashioned bank teller's window, rent their skates at the "Wheel House," but skate on a thoroughly modern epoxy-coated rink floor to music from 76 stereophonic speakers.

With names like "Great Skate," "Hot Wheels," and "The Wheel Thing," roller rinks are getting "with it." They still feature traditional favorites like "Trios," and "Couples Only," and even the ever-popular skate-along tune from the '40s, "The Hokey Pokey," but they also offer roller disco dancing to psychedelic light shows; and for skaters from the Boy and Girl Scouts who jam in after school to the teenagers who take over on Saturday afternoon, and the adults who come by on Saturday night, the neighborhood roller rink is the "in" place to join "what's happening" in the '70s.

At Downey Skate-o-Rama, you feel like you're skating in a park.

Downey Skate-o-Rama

Today's modern skating arenas are a far cry from the roller rinks of yesteryear.

RECHARGE

Chicago Skate Company

Chapter 8

Swinging at the

Roller Disco

Starlight

Bruce Hazelton

Floor guard Ron Bass is into "roller acrobatics."

Cruising down Rosecrans Boulevard in Gardena, California, on a quiet Monday night: gas stations... supermarkets... used car lots. If you weren't on the look-out, you'd miss the Starlight completely. No neon proclamation lights up the sky, but finally, there it is, a 25-year-old airplane hangar in the middle of nowhere, the hand-painted sign over the door: "Roller Skating."

The barrel-vaulted room inside is quiet and empty. Three pinball machines flicker in the corner. But the huge floor extends an invitation—this lovingly worn, black-smudged, and positively irresistible all-maple hardwood floor, just *made* for roller skates. And that's the big attraction—that's what inspired *roller disco* here at the Starlight, long before it caught on in up-to-date roller rinks throughout America.

At seven p.m., the floor guards and popcorn girls have the Starlight to themselves, and with the excuse of sweeping the floor, they jostle on skates over the broom, doing a kind of dance with it—sweeping—sweeping—spinning their wheels and sweeping. Larry Smith rolls over to the disco jockey booth and sends the Temptations blasting off the walls. Larry came out to L.A. from Detroit last year to join his half-brother, Don Harris, who had been doing a lively business at the Starlight since 1974, with skate dancers jiving to tunes from the old jukebox. Larry added psychedelic lights to lend a flash of magic and dusted off the Starlight's stereo system, jolting the place into a roller rocker fantasyland. Now, he spins the disks himself every night, turning skaters on with hot rock and roll, and cooling them down with mellow soul

Bruce Hazelton

Bruce Hazelton

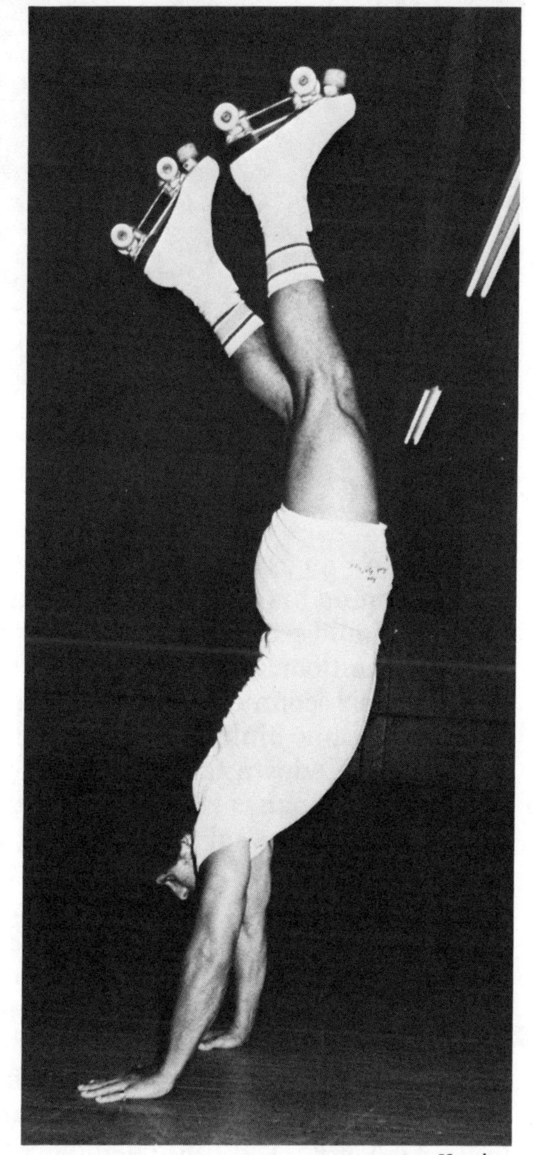

Bruce Hazelton

Bruce Hazelton

Anyone can learn to do the "Freak."

sounds. He's as expert with the floor guard's whistle around his neck as he is with the mike, and you should see him skate! Larry swooshes out onto the floor, sending the girls hustling behind their counter, and then the Pink Panther, in his pink cotton-covered skates, comes bearing down fast. Thirty-six-year-old Ron Bass, has logged 29 years of skating, and his gym shorts reveal that working here as honcho floor guard every night for the past twelve months has produced thigh muscles a quarterback would envy. With a few more precious minutes alone on the rink, Ron grabs Larry, who hangs onto Ron's bull neck for dear life as Ron goes into his airplane spin, faster and faster, until Larry's feet have left the ground and his legs are flying out behind him. "OOOeee," the first customers through the door wail. "Go, Ron!"

Roller junkies! They've paid their $2.50, and they can't seem to get their wheels on fast enough. Some haggle over sizes at the skate rental counter—others fuel up at the snack bar. And once Larry performs his wizardry in the control booth, they explode onto the floor to James Brown wailing over a throbbing guitar. Tonight's the night: once they're up on three inches of wheels, these regulars who mainline skating will cut their own shapes in the thick blur of bodies and let their spirits soar. Don Harris boasts that the same crowd has been skating here for years, so an evening at the Starlight is like going to a big friendly bash. For most, it's a three- or four- or even seven-night-a-week habit. If they don't skate, their feet hurt! And they pride themselves on

Larry Smith and Mr. DeeJay "get down."

Mr. DeeJay perfects his "ankle flop."

Bruce Hazelton

Derrald Gaines can do *any* kind of splits.

Bruce Hazelton

individuality, get high on each other's innovations. Call it skate dancing—the ultimate disco on wheels—or just far-out, unorthodox, but *extraordinary* roller-skating. It's fast, it's slick, and it's captivating.

By eight o'clock, the ribbon of humanity whipping around the floor has created a cold wind—the Starlight has become an ice rink in the dead of winter. But no one complains, the sweat-slick bodies creating their own heat, rocking and rolling at 20 miles an hour. And the Supremes provide an avalanche of music. Urethane wheels purr on the maple, with the occasional snarl of metal as someone out there goes for something *spectacular. Amazing. Sensational.* Round and round the roller rockers sway, with every stroke a knee bounce, every push and glide an elbow pop. They're high-stepping and side-stepping—slide—jump—and high-kicking. And nobody falls down. *Nobody.* Everybody's safe in the beat.

Mr. DeeJay flies on by, a 23-year-old confirmed victim of skate fever. Harry Murry works the Disco Showcase Discotheque five nights a week, but on evenings off, he's out in front of the Starlight at 7:30, a hot pair of roller skates burning up his hands. "You can dance on your feet any old time," the cat insists, "but skating's somethin' different. Man, you can *glide*!" And Mr. DeeJay goes for it, shooting up into the air in skyborne splits, coming down *hard, bang,* on the inside of his ankles. Out in the center of the rink now, the music moves him ("*You are . . . the best of my love . . .*"). He's teaching the "Freak:" side step—one—two—pivot around on the toe stop—three—swoop down and touch your

Bruce Hazelton

toe—twist to the other side....

Derrald Gaines is perfecting his stride nearby. He's into *smooth* skating, and he can't resist Mr. DeeJay's challenge. They make room in the middle for Derrald, whose casual look—boots unlaced down to the ankles—is deceiving. This 20-year-old college student can do his own thing with the best of them. As fingers snap with the beat, Derrald does the heel splits...the sideway splits ...and then double-clutches into a spin. "Get it on!" the crowd yells. Derrald can spin faster than anyone tonight.

"Ladies, clear the floor!" Larry booms over the PA, and wheels rumble like bowling balls as the ladies go off. "Men only" begins. "Function at the Junction" blares with an up-tempo beat, and the cats kick out, rippling and crackling, picking up speed until the wind in the Starlight approaches hurricane velocity. They're flying—*flying*—an uninterrupted gale without beginning or end!

Homey's in from the Big Apple, watching on the sidelines. He's here to check out the roller action on the Coast, still wearing a glittery T-shirt from his high times with the original Roller Rockers, who put disco skating on Broadway. And tonight, at the Starlight, Homey Perkins is impressed. "These dudes can get *down*. They're *travelin'*. It's enough to make you cry!"

"All Skate!" ("*Dancing, dancing, dancing with the beat...*") And who's *this* new lady? *This* lady's a cat: Beverly Thompson stretches sensuously, her silver lamé halter top sparkling under the colored lights. Arms up,

Beverly Thompson moves like a cat.

All photographs credited to Bruce Hazelton

flashing a Diana Ross smile, she moves so *smooth*—you'd think she was rocking and rolling on a conveyor belt. *So smooth*—hands on hips—*so high*—arms to the sky—*head back*—feel the beat... (*"Dancing, dancing, dancing with the beat..."*)

The whistle! "Couples Backwards Skating Only!" Suddenly, as the lights dim down low, there's a race to skate with Beverly. The Rolls-Royce swings with "Do the Dance," and Derrald cuts over first. No. It's Mr. DeeJay who encircles her waist with his arm, his smile matching her own. And then they're flowing with the rhythm—gliding up, down, knee-bouncing along in the *ultimate*—skating backwards, bodies barely touching but in perfect harmony, their own force-field protecting them—so effortless, so beautiful, so smooth...

"Johnny just came in!" The word is out. "Johnny's lacing up his skates right now!" Here he is, five-slapping through the railbirds. Then he's blown out of a cannon onto the rink. ("*Walking in rhythm, moving along...*") Everyone turns to watch a legend: this 30-year-old wizard on wheels who defies Newton's laws, who can barrel along at 20 miles per hour and stop on a dime, who can skate on his front wheels *or* his back—this skating madman who refuses to wear toe stops. Johnny Pool logs hundreds of miles in his car every week, his pair of skates on the front seat beside him, so that he can skate as many rinks as he can from Cucamonga to San Diego. Ten years a roller freak, tonight he shines at the Starlight. ("*Movin' to the music, trying to move on...*") Criss-cross, criss-cross, his skates whoosh front and back, first the right, then the left, his feet never leaving the ground... and he's *smiling*, Johnny never stops *smiling*, not even when he zooms down into the splits around the corner and pulls his legs up just in time for a blast-off into the straightaway—on his *front wheels*. The man is gliding on his *front wheels*! Now he's flipped completely, doing a handstand, as the waves of skaters part around him, and he jumps down, laying five on the honey-smooth floor. Now he's *balancing, balancing*, Johnny's racing on his *outside edges*. "OOooee" they're shouting. "Watch him go for it! Look at that *face*! That's Johnny!" And Johnny's smiling all right, as he tap-dances "*clik clik clack*" on the maple. ("*Thinking about my baby. Trying to move on...*) He grabs a female partner, snaking among the others... Johnny's getting hot.... He can't stay close to his girl.... She's his pivot—The home base for his high-flying roller romping....

And the beat picks up... and the floor goes on forever....

Sharon Boorstin

FROM ROLLER SKATING TO ROLLER DISCO

If you can skate—and you can dance—then you can be a roller rocker. There's really not much to it. The disco music alone will teach you how—just let your body sway to its rhythm.

- Skate with a bounce. Gliding along, keep knees bent, and bounce up and down on each leg in turn, with the beat of the music. (Disco music has a steady rhythm and pulsates on the second and fourth beats.)
- Thrust hips to the side as you shift weight from one leg to the other.
- Keep elbows close to your waist, hands in front.
- Bounce your head, move your arms, and snap your fingers to the rhythm.

Disco Skate with a Partner

As in regular dancing, with partners facing each other, the skater moving forward directs the backwards skater. Each does steps with opposite feet.

To skate side by side and close together, the boy keeps slightly in back, with both partners' hands on the girl's waist. Both do steps with the same feet.

Johnny Pool can skate on his front wheels or his back.

Sharon Boosrstin

Sharon Boorstin

Sharon Boorstin

DISCO SKATING SPECIALTIES

ANKLE FLOP

1. Shift weight onto inside edges, balancing with arms, bending knees.
2. Drop onto inside of ankles. Jump back up into skating position. (Those with weak ankles may find it a cinch to fold in on their ankles, but they find it difficult to bounce back up onto the wheels.)

Sharon Boorstin

Ankle flop

Sharon Boorstin

Sharon Boorstin

High kick

HEEL SPLITS

1. Arms out for balance, skates pointed out, heels together and knees bent, roll skates out with weight on back wheels. Keep tight control with thighs, until legs are two to three feet apart and front wheels are off the ground. (You can rest on your heels.)
2. Pull legs back together, shifting weight evenly over all eight wheels.

HIGH KICK

1. Right arm up, raise up on right toe stop (leaning forward slightly).
2. Kick left leg straight up, toe pointed, using both arms for balance, with weight on right toe stop.

Sharon Boorstin

Heel splits
(Maurice Cooke)

THE PONY

The Pony can be done with or without a partner, and steps can be repeated as many times as you'd like, in any order. Vary arm positions, and be sure to emphasize the hip thrust each time you change legs for the "Grapevine."

1. Knees bent, tip forward up onto toe stops, arms in front for balance.
2. Holding imaginary reins, make little jumps up and down, "galloping" to the beat of the music on toe stops. (Add clicking sounds with tongue against teeth.)
3. Shift weight to right side with a thrust of

Sharon Boorstin

the hips, arms to left.

4. Put weight on right skate, balance on right toe-stop, and roll left skate out in front or to the side in the "Grapevine" step—letting it roll out with weight on back wheels, and pulling it back. (Roll it forward and back a few times. The "Grapevine" can be done rolling forward on front or back wheels.)
5. Shift weight to left skate, go up onto left toe stop, and roll right foot out with weight on back wheels in the "Grapevine," and pull it back. Repeat "Grapevine" on front wheels.
6. Pivot around on toe stop to face opposite direction and repeat dance.

THE BUMP

A dance for two partners with improvised "bumps" on the beat. Use toe stops to help balance.

1. Partners side by side, side-step two beats to left, then two to right, shifting weight with an exaggerated swing of the hips.

Sharon Boorstin

2. Bump hips, legs, elbows, and backsides together as you continue the side-step movement, bending knees so you go low to floor and come up again. Circle around each other as you continue.

Chapter 9

Merrily We Roll

The Outdoor Skating Scene—Sunday in Venice --

Along

Marilyn Sanders

Sharon Boorstin

On a crowded Sunday afternoon, you have to wait your turn to rent roller skates.

It's another balmy Sunday afternoon in Southern California. Sailboats flicker in a regatta out of the Marina del Rey, and nearby, at the funky oceanfront community of Venice, the beach is alive with surfers, swimmers, and sybaritic sunbathers. But the action isn't reserved to the sea and the sand: on the two-mile strip of asphalt bordering the beach, musicians play, artists hawk their crafts, and Sunday strollers enjoy the local color. In front of Cheapskates, 50 roller addicts stand in their stocking feet waiting their turn in line to rent roller skates. And Cheapskates' owner, Jeffrey Rosenberg, is enjoying the frenzy of exchanging sneakers for skates over the counter—Sunday is his biggest day.

Jeff has turned roller rags into roller riches, setting off the outdoor skating craze that began in Venice and soon took the nation by storm. While a student at Santa Monica College, Jeff roller-skated to class and toyed with the idea of renting skates to the tourists who walked along the Venice boardwalk on Sundays. His friends thought he was crazy, but Jeff played out a hunch, saving money until he could buy 25 pairs of used roller skates. Though the salesman advised him to stock up on children's sizes, Jeff knew better: Southern California's health-conscious adults will try anything that promises good exercise. And one summer day in 1976, he parked his van next to the boardwalk and put up a sign: "Roller skates $1.00 an hour."

Women in their late teens and twenties were the first to take the bait, and once they were hooked, men were soon wheeling along to catch up with them. So, outdoor roller-skating, like bicycle-riding an activity once strictly for the kiddies, became the "in" Sunday sport for grown-ups. Today, Jeff has two Cheapskates shops stocked with 450 pairs of rental skates, and a mail-order business offering a complete line of roller-skating equipment and "roller rags" to outfit the fashionable skater. And this Sunday, like any sunny Sunday throughout the year, Jeff will have to be on his toes; everyone seems to have the urge to go roller-skating....

Sharon Boorstin

Sharon Boorstin

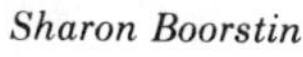

Moving to music makes it all worthwhile for James Truitt and "Red" Jimmy Mitchell, who "do their Venice thing" slow and easy to rhythm and blues, and swing into backwards racing when the beat picks up....

And Gerald Estrin, a distinguished 56-year-old UCLA professor, is just getting his "roller legs." He hasn't been on roller skates in 30 years, but today he's out here with his wife and daughter, staying, already, pretty much right on course. "After all," he boasts, "I was quite a whiz in my day—drove the storekeepers crazy skating around 204th Street where I grew up in the Bronx. It feels terrific to be back on wheels again." "Yes," his wife chimes in, "the family that skates together..."

The storekeepers in Venice don't mind the skaters at all. In fact, many of them have taken to wheels themselves! Terra Jenett wears her skates all day, custom-designing

Marilyn Sanders

Sharon Boorstin

Gerald Estrin is just getting his "roller legs". He hasn't been on skates in 30 years!

Sharon Boorstin

Decking out in "roller rags" is half the fun of skating.

Sharon Boorstin

Sharon Boorstin

James Truitt and "Red" Jimmy Mitchell like to bring their music along with them.

The Venice Beach offers sun, sand, surf—and free-wheeling along the boardwalk.

Sharon Boorstin

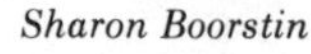
Sharon Boorstin

Sharon Boorstin

Many of those who have to *work* along the boardwalk do it on roller skates.

air-brushed roller fashions (pastel-decorated T-shirts and skate covers) and selling them to shoppers. And after closing time at dusk, she and her boyfriend sometimes skate until two or three in the morning. At a restaurant called "Alice in Veniceland," Tisha Suckler is waitress on wheels to skaters who stop by for a roast turkey leg or a fresh lemonade....

But even customers who are famished stop eating long enough to get a good look

Sharon Boorstin

Doug Waters takes a daily stroll on his ice-hockey training skates.

Sharon Boorstin

when Doug Waters happens by. He draws as many stares on the boardwalk as he would if he were wearing *ice* skates. That's what it *looks* like he's wearing as he glides along on his *very unusual* roller skates. The four narrow polyurethane wheels, lined up in a straight row, look like the blade on an ice skate. And Doug takes a spin on them every day of the week. "Once you get the hang of balancing on these ice hockey training skates," he insists, "you can cut a pretty fancy figure. . . ."

The smooth cement strip leading off the bike path by the Venice Pavilion is jumping: the *serious* skaters are doing some *serious* skating. Greg Watts is out here for his hour of daily practice. He's invented a backwards 360, and he wants to show off his donkey kick: a knee-bending jump up, popping his toes into his behind—just like a donkey. "The slight incline makes it easier to work out here," says Steve Parfet, demonstrating a perfect figure eight in a heels-together, knees-bent "surf-side" position. But Ellen Margolin seems to be the most popular today. Practicing some of the old routines she used to do on ice skates, and wearing a form-hugging leotard, she draws onlookers admiring her figures and her figure.

Sharon Boorstin

Steve Parfet can do an odd-looking figure eight.

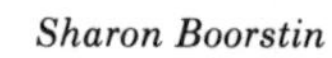

Greg Watts does a "donkey kick."

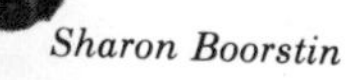

Sharon Boorstin

But Ellen Margolin has the biggest audience.

Sharon Boorstin

Half-court roller polo is big in Venice.

The Martians have landed! In the court by the flagpoles, some weird-looking guys are shuffling around on wheels: with thick pads on their chests and elbows, white plastic shin guards, hard helmets and mouth plates, they look like they're from outer space. The skaters, ranging from 13 to 33, are playing half-court roller hockey, a fast and slick game that can be set up in a small concrete area like this one. A group of Venice roller addicts started knocking a puck around last summer, and now they make it a regular Sunday afternoon event—two three-man teams and one goalie. (See rules for half-court roller hockey at the end of the chapter.)

The owner of the Sidewalk Café is having a fit: "Who stole my garbage cans?" A husky skater makes off with the last one, laying it next to six others he has carefully arranged on the bike path. Brad Dunton, a 22-year-old

Brad Dunton is breaking the garbage-can jumping record . . .

. . . until the cops put a stop to it . . .

Sharon Boorstin

Sharon Boorstin

Marine, is out to break a record—if he doesn't break his neck. Last spring he cleared a spectacular 15 feet, eight inches, jumping over eight beer kegs, and now he wants to make it over eight "Keep Venice Clean" garbage cans.

Setting records is nothing new to Brad. He won Cheapskates' Easter race from Venice to the Santa Monica pier last year—two miles in eight minutes; and in 1976, he broke the world skating marathon record of 183 hours, 7 minutes, by staying on his wheels for 8 days, 9 hours, and 13 minutes. With only two free hours for showering and sleeping after every 24 skated in the Sherman Square Rink, he was so strung out by the end of his stint, he ended up spending two days recuperating in the hospital!

So far this afternoon, he has made it over six garbage cans, and now he measures off the seven garbage cans in a row: 20 feet, more or less. The countdown begins. Brad clears away

...so Brad finds other tricks to occupy his time—like the "sideways shoot-the-duck."

stray grass and sand on the approach route and moves back for the takeoff. Bike riders pause to watch, photographers aim their cameras, as the six foot four-inch skater comes barreling along, picking up speed until his toe stops practically jam against the first garbage can in the line. Then, arms up, knees pulled in tight, WHOOSH! Brad sails over all seven cans, without even a clank of wheels on metal. Superman! *BAM!* He lands *hard*, and cruises to a smooth stop as the enthusiastic crowd bursts into a round of applause.

Brad's not ready to give up yet. He's searching around for another "Keep Venice Clean" and skates over to nab one from the hockey goal. But suddenly, the 200 fans fall back as an L.A. policeman swaggers over to see what's up: garbage cans laid side by side? That's tampering with city property. Skating on the bike path? A serious violation of the vehicle code—roller skaters are pedestrians, subject to a $20 fine if caught on the cement reserved for bicycles. Sorry. Only a leather-neck would try something like this, the cop groans, letting Brad off with a warning and sending him to put the cans back where they belong. Oh well, Brad sighs, there are other world records on top: he still plans to skate all the way across the country, breaking the 64-day record set in 1974. In the meantime, he settles for a nice, safe spot where he can practice another of his specialties, the "sideways shoot the duck"—skating on one foot, body low and parallel to the ground, his ear a hair's breadth away from the asphalt....

Sharon Boorstin

Fred Blood can run the slalom course sideways.

Sharon Boorstin

Sandy Westbrook roller-skates on a skateboard.

Down the coast, just south of the marina, the four-mile "Strand" that fronts the beach between Redondo and Manhattan shimmers with skaters who make wheeling in Venice look like child's play. City law here was changed to give roller skaters free access to the smooth cement bike path. And every weekend, they make the most of it.

Early in the morning, slalom cones mark a course in front of Wild Wheels skate shop. The kids who gather have come to try their hand at "hot-dog" skating. Fred Blood is here (see Chapter XI), and so are a dozen other teenagers, outfitted in shorts, knee pads, and wearing skates with soft red Kryptonic wheels. They all have their own style as they maneuver the slalom. Fred zooms along in a perfect "surf-side" position. Sandy Westbrook runs the course backwards, smoothly criss-crossing her legs as if there were no cones to knock over at all (and none go over!). Then she makes a quick, teetering try at roller-skating on a skateboard.

Fred wants to try some jumps, and instead of resorting to garbage cans, convinces Wild Wheels' owner, Ray Tate, to have a seat right in the middle of the Strand. Twenty feet away, Fred takes off, building up speed and momentum in the approach, and then it's UP UP in a flash, as his wheels barely clear the wisps of hair blowing in the breeze—whisps of hair on Ray's no longer carefully-coiffed head! "Just another hard day at the beach," Ray sighs...

Bruce Hazelton

Fred Blood tries some jumps.

Bruce Hazelton

Sharon Boorstin

OUTDOOR SKATING IN YOUR HOMETOWN

1. City parks offer sidewalks and bike paths, and in many parks where cars are prohibited on Sundays, you can skate safely in the street. (Golden Gate in San Francisco and Central Park in New York City are good examples.)
2. Check city laws regarding roller-skating on lanes marked off for bicycles on city streets.
3. A cement parking lot or parking structure that is crowded with cars during the week may be an empty cement roller rink on Sunday.
4. A school playground that is usually full of screaming children can be an ideal spot for roller games on the weekend. (See list below.)
5. City sidewalks in downtown shopping areas—or on shopping center plazas—may provide roller skaters clear sailing on Sundays.

Bruce Hazelton

GAMES TO MAKE OUTDOOR SKATING MORE FUN

1. Set up a slalom course: use cones, milk cartons, cardboard boxes, garbage cans. Decrease the space between them after each run-through.
2. Try doing the limbo on roller skates, lowering the limbo stick after each try.
3. Play Frisbee on skates.
4. Try playing baseball—or basketball—on roller skates.
5. Set up jumps—over cardboard boxes, chairs—but be sure you have a nice grassy spot for a safe, happy landing.
6. Broom polo: use ordinary kitchen brooms and any makeshift "puck" you can find.
7. Street soccer: maneuver the ball or puck with your skates.
8. Half-court roller hockey: You can play this miniaturized version of roller hockey in an area no larger than 60 x 80 feet. You need only one goal (set up garbage cans to mark it off), one goalie, and two teams of three players each. Use a plastic or rubber air-filled puck. Try to find an area to play in that is enclosed on three sides with walls or boards (or even street curbs), so that you can play the puck off them. The defending team must get the puck outside the playing area to take possession and become the attacking team. Play to games of 5 points each.

Chapter 10

Rolling into the

The World of Competitive Skating

RSROA

Big Time

At a local Junior Olympics, contestants in the figure-eights division are judged on their accuracy in following the path marked on the floor. . . . And nobody gives up just because of falling down.

Sharon Boorstin

Sharon Boorstin

World Pairs Champions, Karen Mejia and Ray Chappata, have elevated roller-skating into art.

A BEGINNING: THE LOCAL JUNIOR OLYMPICS

Doors at the Sherman Square Roller Rink in Southern California's San Fernando Valley will open any minute, and already, at 5:45 a.m. on a chilly Sunday in November, a crowd is impatient to get in. Several hundred Junior Olympics contenders had to roll out of bed long before dawn to make it here on time. But no one looks bleary-eyed—except perhaps for some of the dutiful mothers and fathers who have driven their children here from as far away as Santa Barbara.

Once inside, the skates are laced tight, the wheels adjusted, and skaters five years old and up fight off the jitters as they slip into their costumes. Today, they will be vying for medals and trophies in several categories. *Figure Eights* come first: the kids are judged on their accuracy in following the circles marked on the floor. Then, the *Dance Competition* finds four contestants at a time sharing the floor, performing one of the traditional roller waltzes, tangos, or foxtrots, set to organ music. But the long-awaited event is the *Freestyle*, when the most accomplished finalists take their turn, one at a time, to demonstrate their skating grace and expertise in an original dance of glides, spins, and complicated skating routines they have carefully choreographed to their favorite tunes—from "Lara's Theme" to "Star Wars." In the Juvenile division, each contender executes camel spins, cartwheels, and even the splits, with all the finesse of a freewheeling miniature Dorothy Hamill, and nobody gives up just because he or she falls down. Competition is fierce, and after several elimination rounds, proud winners will go home with bronze, silver, and gold medals.

With dedication—and at least three hours of practice a day—these junior skaters may move on to skate in regional and later national or even international competitions, joining the over one million roller skaters who have vied in amateur competition since it was organized in 1937.

BALLET ON WHEELS—ARTISTIC ROLLER-SKATING

With the strumming of a balalaika, a Russian folk song strikes up, and out of the darkness two figures glide into a brightly lit arena. They pause, pirouette, then trace a turn as the man gracefully lifts his partner into the air above him, her free leg kicking high. The crowd roars its approval as Karen Mejia and Ray Chappata, both 21, perform the head-turning finale of their dance on wheels to win the 1977 World Freestyle Roller Skate Dance Competition in Montreal.

This is *freestyle* roller-skating at its most dazzling—the climax of many painstaking hours of skillful choreography and wearying practice. An award-winning dance is a harmonious blend of difficult and inventive move-

RSROA

Waltz position

ments, an effective use of floor space, and a creative interpretation of music. The skaters must complement each other in their body movements, so that each step becomes an organic part of their dance together. Their skating routine must display their skill in as many different dance positions and sequences of steps as possible, to create a unique, rhythmic performance the audience will remember long after the music fades.

Ray Chappata and Karen Mejia have developed *pairs skating* to a fine art, introducing fresh innovations: movements from classical ballet, lively Eastern European music, and trend-setting costumes (50 homemade outfits each that range from peasant dress to space suits). Ray is particularly enthusiastic about combining ballet and roller-skating, for he is an accomplished professional dancer as well as skater. To Ray, "making a skating program is like painting a picture—the floor is your canvas, the music is your color, and your body is the painting brush. As in painting, you have the problem of deciding how to fill the floor with innovative and interesting movements that are aesthetically appealing to the eye and blend to create a whole."

Ray and Karen often put in up to ten hours of practice a day before a big tournament, and they train with all the intensity of athletes preparing for contact sports. "I could press weights for strength," admits Ray, "but I found lifting Karen is better." (She is five feet, and 95 pounds, and he is five feet ten inches, and 150 pounds.) And when Ray picks Karen up, it looks easy—even in twist lifts, swing lifts, and elaborate around-the-back axles.

For years, top *artistic skaters* have contended that the moves and routines they master with their wheels on wooden floors easily surpass what ice skaters do with their blades, and considering the wheels weigh five pounds each to the ice skate blades' two, that is quite an achievement. Two-time world champion Natalie Dunn of Bakersfield, California, says, "Take triple jumps, for example. Only recently, there have been a few ice skaters who could do triple jumps. But roller

Open position

Illustrations by Marsha Eva Gold

skaters have been doing triple jumps for years! They're old hat with us. We feel it's about time we got credit for performing in a sport that's every bit as good as, if not better than, ice-skating."

Roller-skating's time has finally come. More than 40 countries now participate in international competition, and for the first time, the sport will be included in the 1979 Pan American Games. With the high tide of enthusiasm and participation in roller-skating, there seems little doubt that it will be included in the 1984 summer Olympics.

How to Get It On

So you want to become a roller ballerina? Start at your local skating arena. Any rink that belongs to the Roller Skating Rink Operator's Association offers classes and private lessons in the traditional dances performed in competition, including those with such exotic names as the Glide waltz, the Siesta tango, and the Fascination foxtrot. You can proceed at your own pace, put in as many hours a week as you choose, and you'll earn RSROA bronze and silver proficiency medals as you perfect each dance. With or without a partner, you can learn all the spins, jumps, and sequences of steps required to create your own freestyle dance (and you can earn proficiency medals in the freestyle category as well). As a member of your rink's skating club, you can enter local, regional, and then—who knows—even national competition.

It Takes Two to Tango

As in dancing, skating with a partner is a way to double your pleasure. And it's easy: the music's tempo determines the timing of the steps, and the melody governs the style, and the only part you have to get right is skating close together without bumping into one another.

With both people skating forward in the *Open Position*, the man's right hand is on the lady's right hip, her right hand over his. The lady's left hand extends across her partner and is held in his left hand.

For the *Waltz Position*, the partners skate face-to-face, one moving forward, the other

Speed skaters eight years old and younger can enter "Primary" division races.

Sharon Boorstin

Learning to skate figures is a good way to start a career in competitive skating.

backward. The lady's left hand is on the man's right shoulder. His right hand is on her back. Their opposite hands are extended to the side and held hand-in-hand.

FIGURE SKATING

A competitive, or *classic figure eight* is composed of two circles which form an eight together. Executing a roller-skating figure eight is much like cutting one with a blade on ice, except here, the figure is painted on the floor, and the skater traces it with his wheels. For each of the figures, the skater begins on the right foot at the intersection of the two circles, and skates a complete circle on each foot, ideally making it all the way around on one stroke.

Skating figures may be one of the best ways to begin a competitive skating career, for even the greenest beginners can learn to trace a figure eight, and as they gain the control necessary to perform one, they are sharpening their balance and coordination—essential for skating in the big arena. In fact, figure-skating is considered so essential to the overall assessment of a skater's ability that in international freestyle competition compulsory figure eights comprise the elimination round, and only the top eight winners in the figure division are allowed to perform in the freestyle final event. Then, each contestant's figure-skating score is added to his freestyle score to determine the overall champion.

RSROA

Chris Snyder is twice winner of the Senior Men's Speed Championship.

RSROA

RSROA

RSROA

Roller hockey is fast and furious.

SPEED SKATING

Speed roller-skating attracts one third of all registered competitive roller skaters, who vie in local, regional, and national matches. Races are held on 16-lap tracks, usually indoors in the United States, though outdoor (sometimes banked) tracks are popular in Italy and other European countries.

The rules of speed skating have changed little since it was organized on a national level in 1937, but the equipment has been modernized so that today, skaters can race much faster than they used to. Lightweight, sure-gripping sycamore and pine wheels have replaced the slower maple wood wheels, and skate plates now have holes drilled in them, creating a strong but lighter weight support.

Coated with epoxy, wood floors are now faster and safer than they used to be. But still, controversy rages about whether speed skaters perform better on loose or sealed bearings. Some feel the loose bearings give a faster roll in the takeoff, but others believe precision bearings are superior for a consistent, smooth roll.

Among the nine areas of speed skating, divisions range from Senior Men's (over age 18), with 1000, 1500, 3000, and 5000-meter races, down to Primary Boys or Girls (under age 8) going 200, 300, and 400-meter distances. Two and four-man teams compete in *relay speed races*: A typical senior mixed relay (with male and female team members) has each team member skating 500 meters twice in a 4000-meter race.

Speed skating is a far cry from Roller Derby—the contestants take it seriously and train hard for every race. A perfect example of a dedicated roller racer: Chris Snyder, 22, of Irving, Texas, in 1974 and 1977, winner of the Senior Men's Speed Championship. Skating has always been a major part of Chris's life since the age of three. His two brothers and sister are also competitive skaters, and all four children learned to master their wheels at their father's roller rink. Before winning his championship, Chris trained indoors at the rink three times a week, usually two to three hours each day, and put in ten to twenty miles outdoors whenever the weather permitted. The time spent working out paid off: In 1977, Chris set a record in the 3000-meter race with a time of 6:21.1, and also in the 5000-meter race with a time of 10:33.2.

Tips for the Beginning Roller Racer

Roller speed-skating requires split-second timing, calculations made to the fraction of an inch, and physical conditioning surpassing that needed for other forms of competitive roller-skating. Advice to budding speedsters:

1. Learn proper timing: To avoid the pylons at the four corners of the track, you must pass your opponents well before you're out of the straightaway.
2. Practice pacing: Gain endurance by skating long stretches at an even clip, crouched low, your body one to one and a half feet lower than a normal erect position.
3. Practice crossing right foot over left in a rhythmic, easy, flowing motion, so that you will be able to corner with as much ease as when you skate down the straightaway. Keep weight on right foot as you round the corners.
4. Learn to win at the start: Balance yourself with weight over the starting line, leaning forward, fists clenched, and be prepared to explode over the line with the gun, arms and feet moving rapidly from the first stroke. Practice by running on your toe stops, as low to the floor as possible.
5. Perhaps the hardest trick in racing is completing a pass without fouling another skater. With little room on the narrow track, you must overtake the racer ahead of you in time to negotiate the turn. To avoid

being passed yourself, put on a burst of speed in the straightaway and "shadow" the skater in front of you—without leaving room for an opponent to wedge in from behind.

6. Most important: Psych yourself up to win. Assume that everyone behind you wants to pass you—and don't let them!

ROLLER HOCKEY

In the 1890s, roller polo was the rage, and after a lull in popularity, it showed up during the '20s as roller hockey on city playgrounds. Today, with the tremendous enthusiasm for professional ice hockey, its roller cousin is attracting skaters who love the year-round thrill of this rugged game. You'll see half-court games from Manhattan streets to California parking lots, and full-court roller hockey in roller rinks across the nation. The Hockey Skating Union, under the U.S. Amateur Confederation, has organized clubs into national leagues, with divisions for both men and women, ranging from Midget (players under age ten), to Seniors (no age limit).

Ball hockey, played with a nine-inch ball, is the official roller hockey game in international tournaments. But both ball hockey and *puck hockey* are played in national competition. And both games are fast and furious: two five-man teams, using wooden hockey sticks, scrap to fire the ball or plastic puck into the opponent's goal cage. Wearing colorful padded uniforms, the players' daring-do on wheels keeps audiences on the edge of their seats.

Check with the *Roller Skating Rink Operators Association—7700 "A" Street, Lincoln, Nebraska*—to find a rink near you that offers a roller hockey club to watch, or join yourself. (See description of half-court hockey rules on page 133.)

Chorus Line on Wheels: The Gold Skate Classic

What the Ice Capades is to professional ice-skating, the Gold Skate Classic is to amateur roller-skating. In fact, many of the skaters who enter regional and national competitions in dance and freestyle roller-skating look forward most to performing in this special annual extravaganza.

Every February, in Bakersfield, California, over a thousand amateur roller skaters from clubs throughout the West vie in a two-day roller-skating spectacular, with singles and couples performing elaborate routines. Their costumes are as sensational as the themes—from "Lovers' Quarrel" to "Scheherazade." Skaters are judged for roller-skating expertise, for interpretation of theme, for costumes, music, and most important of all, for *showmanship*. The highlight of the weekend: the group numbers, where sometimes as many as 120 skaters in stunning costumes dance on wheels with all the pizzazz of a Broadway chorus line.

Contestants in the Gold Skate Classic are judged on costumes and showmanship as well as on their skating expertise.

Warren Pope

Costumes and theme are as important as the skating in the Gold Skate Classic.

RSROA

RSROA

Chapter II

Skating in the

Invading the Skateboard Park

Sky

Bruce Hazelton

The "surf-side" position is essential for good balance on the curved concrete surfaces of a skateboard park.

At three p.m. on a sunny day in Torrance, California, teenagers hop on their bikes at Torrance High and clear out. Instead of heading for home, they light out for Skateboard World where, boards and safety equipment in tow, they pay their $2.50 for two hours in a skateboarders' paradise: a two-and-a-half-acre park with six swimming-pool-shaped concrete paths of varying lengths, heights, and angles of curvature. But while they're busy tightening the bolts on their trucks and sanding their board surfaces in preparation, one 15-year-old is way ahead of them. Fred Blood prefers *wearing* his wheels on his feet, and he's laced into super-lightweight nylon-and-vinyl skates with wide oval polyurethane wheels. On these "radical" outdoor roller skates, Fred can trounce even the most outrageous skateboarders. And he's fast on his way to setting a new trend.

The curly-headed blond dons his crash helmet, adjusts his knee and elbow pads, and eases his hands into a heavy pair of leather gloves. First, he warms up in the "freestyle" area, skating back and forth in the "surf-side" position—knees bent, heels together, legs apart and toes pointed in opposite directions. After a few practice runs up the side of the curving wall and back down, Fred is ready for a challenge. The skateboarders respectfully step aside to allow him first crack at the most hair-raising course of all—the "half-pipe." A pause at the top to survey the run, then Fred dives into the chute and zooms down the curving concrete toboggan course, snaking around the first curve, into the second, building up momentum and speed. Rounding the third bend, he reaches a broad bowl with sloping walls seven feet high. Left foot leading in the "surf-side" position, he zips up one wall, his arms poised shoulder-high, elbows bent for balance. At the top, facing the bottom of the bowl, he "rides the coping" in a perfect arc, outside wheels barely skirting the lip of the bowl. Left foot still leading, he curves back down the wall. WHOOSH. It's up the other side—to the rim—and this time he *flies out* of the bowl, his body poised in the air two feet above the concrete. He twists into an aerial about-face, then lands on the side of the wall, left foot still leading, for another glide down and over to the other side. Then it's *up* the other wall for a "fly out" and *another* aerial spectacular—*higher* than the last. The skateboarders watch in admiration as Fred keeps it up: WHOOSH WHOOSH—up one side and back down into the bowl in two seconds flat. He zigzags back and forth without missing a beat, as even and as smooth as a metronome, until, twenty *whooshes* later, he finally begins to wind down. Then, he glides to the end of the run and jumps out onto the grass.

"Far out! Wow, it's like flying—like total weightlessness in outer space!" Fred grins, barely out of breath. "It's even better with music. Sometimes I borrow my friend's earphones when I'm hot. Then I can get even higher." What about wipe-outs? "Oh, I fall Man, roller-skating here is easier than

Bruce Hazelton

skateboarding—and more fun. You can get a lot more radical!"

Fred admits he was into skateboarding a few years back—until he saw the first skateboarding film, *Freewheeling*. What dazzled him in the movie wasn't the skateboarding, but the *roller-skating* by hot-dogger Ken Means. Fred went straight to J.C. Penny, bought himself a $12 pair of roller skates, and never climbed onto his skateboard again. He roller skated daily on the Strand, the Pacific Ocean boardwalk just a short glide away from his house in Hermosa Beach, and soon began trying the jumps and slaloms set up in front of Wild Wheels, the skateboard and roller skate shop there. He was hooked. He put in seven to eight hours a day on his skates, perfecting his techniques in the curved bowls at the skateboard park, until he could "fly out" and complete aerial turns with ease—zapping all the skateboarders and roller skaters combined.

Today, Fred skates professionally in exhibitions, but only on *curved* surfaces. (Going round and round a floor isn't his idea of fun.) Some weekends, he and his friends drive out to Tempe, Arizona, near the Colorado River, where enormous pipes sit on the desert, just waiting for someone to loop-the-loop in them. And Fred is one in a million: Defying the laws of gravity, he can *almost* make it *360 degrees* all the way around.

ROLLER TECHNIQUES FOR THE SKATEBOARD PARK

1. Practice "surf-side" skating on level ground first: toes turned outwards, heels together, feet in a straight line, knees bent. Balance arms out at shoulder level, with elbows up and hands in front. The more you center your weight, the better your maneuverability. (You'll find some pulling in your thigh muscles until they strengthen.) In this position, you can easily and naturally skate in an arc.
2. Move to the skateboard park's *warm-up* area. (It usually has one wall curving up from a level surface.) Build up your momentum skating up and down the level surface until you can thrust up the side of the wall, in "surf-side" position. Skate up to the top, left foot leading, then drop your weight to the right foot, and right foot leading, skate back down. Let your arms find a natural balancing position.
3. After you begin to feel comfortable skating the wall up and back in a straight line, try "riding the coping" (named after the edge of a swimming pool, where skateboarders frolicked before skateboard parks). When you're up at the lip, with plenty of momentum to keep you going, bend into an arc, facing the bottom of the bowl, leading with the foot you came up the side on, and maintain that position until you gently curve back toward the bottom of the bowl,

Bruce Hazelton

still leading with the same foot.

4. Once you can "ride the coping," try adding an "aerial." When you reach the lip of the bowl, leading up the wall with your *right* foot, press your body weight higher, so that your feet actually fly off the wall for a few seconds before you land back on the wall and head down, leading with your *left* foot.
5. Add an "aerial turn": Into your "aerial," twist your body around so that you're facing the bottom of the bowl, assuring that you land first on the *right* foot. Then lead back down into the bowl on it.

Left foot leading, Fred Blood ascends the curved wall.

His feet lift off the wall in an "aerial"...

Bruce Hazelton

...as he pulls his knees up and twists his body around in the air...

Bruce Hazelton

. . . getting ready to land on his left foot . . .

Bruce Hazelton

...and descend the wall...

Bruce Hazelton

. . . only to zip up the opposite wall.

Bruce Hazelton

Fred "rides the coping," his wheels skimming the lip of the bowl.

Bruce Hazelton

Fred Blood finds a gigantic pipe on the desert the perfect spot to go roller-skating.

Bruce Hazelton

Bruce Hazelton

Fred shoots the 17-foot deep "vertibowl" at Paramount Skatepark.

Bruce Hazelton

Fred flies out of the "Pool-Bowl" at Runway Skatepark.

Fred tries his luck on the Pepsi Ramp at the Sidewalk Surfpark in Fountain Valley, Ca.

Bruce Hazelton

Chapter 12

Roller Records

Facts and Figures: Serious, and Not So Serious

FACTS AND FIGURES:

Of the over 20 million Americans roller-skating today, 38.5% are 18 years of age and older, 31.5% are in the 12-17 age bracket, and 30% are under 12 years of age.

* * * * * * *

The average-sized roller-skate wheel (2″ in diameter), turns at a rate of 3,360 rpm.

* * * * * * *

The largest rink in the history of roller-skating was the Grand Hall in London, England. It opened in 1890 and closed in 1912, and had a 68,000-square-foot skating surface. (The average roller rink today covers 14,000 square feet.)

* * * * * * *

Marathon skating: Randy Reed, 21, skated 322 hours and 20 minutes over 13 days, in a Springfield, Oregon, roller rink in 1977.

* * * * * * *

TRANSCONTINENTAL SKATE:

Longest skate: Clint Shaw skated from Victoria, B.C., to St. John's, Newfoundland (4,900 miles), on the Trans-Canadian Highway, from April 1 to November 11, 1967.

Across the U.S.: Clint Shaw skated from New York City to Santa Monica, California (3100 miles), April 1 to May 4, 1974. (His longest one-day stint, 106 miles.)

First woman to skate across the U.S.: (40 years earlier than a man). In 1933, Gerane Withington skated from Oregon to Florida, averaging 12 to 13 miles a day.

* * * * * * *

BARREL JUMP:

Brad Dunton, 21, jumped over eight beer kegs (15′8″) to set a barrel-jumping record in 1977.

* * * * * * *

SPEED RECORDS:

25.78 mph by Giuseppe Cantarella (Italy) on a road in Cantania, Italy, September 28, 1963.

Mile record on a rink: 2 minutes, 25.1 seconds by Gianni Ferretti (Italy.)

Greatest distance in one hour on a closed road circuit: 22 miles, 465 yards. Alberto Civolani (Italy), Bologna, Italy, October 15, 1967.

Greatest distance in one hour on a rink by a woman: 20 miles, 1,355 yards by C. Patricia Barnett (U.K.), skated in London, June 24, 1962.

* * * * * * *

MOST TITLES:

Speed skating: Miss A. Vianello (Italy) with 16 titles between 1953 and 1965.

Pairs skating: Dieter Fingerle (W. Germany) with 4 titles (1959, 1965, 1966, and 1967.)

Figure skating: Karl Heinz Losch with 5 titles (1958, 1959, 1961, 1962, and 1966.)

Roller hockey: Portugal, with 11 world championship titles from 1947 to 1972.

* * * * * * *

MOST AMAZING COMEBACK:

Edgar Watrous, winner of the Mens Singles title in 1955 and 1956, skated in this event the following nine years before regaining his title in 1965.

RSROA

Marriage on roller skates: June 1976: Keri Malone and Berry Delien tied the knot while wearing roller skates at the Ardomore Ches-A-Rena in Cheswick, Pennsylvania. All 16 members of the wedding party were on skates, and the eight bridesmaids wore short skating costumes. The minister performed the ceremony wearing skates as well.

* * * * * * *